A Time of Silence

The Story of a Childhood Holocaust Survivor

Ingrid Epstein Elefant

authorHOUSE®

AuthorHouse™
1663 Liberty Drive
Bloomington, IN 47403
www.authorhouse.com
Phone: 1-800-839-8640

First published by AuthorHouse   3/9/2011

ISBN: 978-1-4520-9880-7 (sc)
ISBN: 978-1-4520-9881-4 (e)
ISBN: 978-1-4520-9879-1 (dj)

Library of Congress Control Number: 2011900802

Printed in the United States of America

This book is dedicated to

My grand parents
William and Agnes Kammen
Righteous Gentiles who protected my life at their own peril
During the Holocaust

And to
My grandchildren
Jason, Sarah, Joshua and Stephanie
Our future

ACKNOWLEDGMENT

I AM MOST GRATEFUL FOR THE HELP and support of so many people, without whom this book would never have come to fruition. To Dr. Stanley Grossman, who saved my injured soul and without whose encouragement I would not have finished this book. To my good friends Rabbi Marim and Paula Charry, whose gentle support helped me to *come out* and tell my story in public for the first time. To Rabbi Charry for being my *rebbe*; teaching, explaining and always helping me to deepen my Judaism. To Paula for being a cherished friend, who helped me with my *mikveh* venture and in general answered many practical household questions to support my new *kashruth* practice. Thank you to Gladys Roth and her wonderful memoir writing group, for their support and tears. To Edith and Peter Robbins, dear friends who never stinted with their help, Edie for reading my manuscript and Pete for helping me navigate the overwhelming maze of publishing. Thank you to Phyllis Brusiloff for her gift of time and talent in editing my manuscript and to Lori Segal Oppenheimer for her gift of proofreading. I am grateful to Irving Roth, Director of the Holocaust Resource Center at Temple Judea, who not only made me one of his cadre of survivors who testify, but helped me accept that my story had value.

I thank my many special friends for being there, loving me and giving me support; Joan Baraf who is always there to love, help and support me, no matter what; Lynn Nemeroff, Sondra Winder; Pamela Rademacher and so many others. Most of all I thank my family for being who they are; my dear husband Jack for his eternal patience and quiet love and support. My wonderful daughters, Ellen Cohen Johnstone and Wendy Eckstein, who enrich my life endlessly and who gave me the greatest gift on earth, my grandchildren, Jason Cohen, Sarah Eckstein, Stephanie Cohen and Joshua Eckstein, who imbue my life with meaning and hope.

INTRODUCTION

THIS IS THE STORY OF GROWING UP in Germany during World War II, my terror during the war and its effect on my life and the racist atrocities of Nazism resulting in my displacement and painful sense of abandonment, guilt and confusion.

This memoir is not necessarily history, since the memory of childhood can be unreliable. The truth and sincerity in my story come from recollections as I gathered them from memory like so many snapshots from an old album, and the impact on me of particular experiences. I write this more than sixty years later and the memories, fears, confusions and yearnings of the child have been filtered through and inevitably censored by the mind of the adult. To the best of my ability, I paint my recollections with the limited color pallet of the child to capture the sense of how I experienced the events around me.

My Mother and Father

Chapter 1
In the Beginning

I, Ingrid Agnes Kammen, was born in Germany in 1936 into a world already dangerously infected by Hitler's manic dreams and promises, which soon became the nightmare of Jews in all of Europe. My Jewish mother married her Catholic sweetheart three years before my birth, causing I know not what kind of turmoil in her parental home for marrying a non-Jew. Her eldest sister had already set a precedent by marrying a Gentile, so I can only conjecture that my grandparents were not quite as shocked when my mother also married out. After I made my entrance into their world, I was promptly baptized in the Catholic Church and dutifully named after my paternal grandmother, Agnes. This became my middle name, making it easier later on to keep such a Catholic sounding name a secret. My first name, Ingrid, is more ubiquitous and I was always grateful to my parents for bestowing it on me.

Of the many unanswered questions that marked a pattern in my life, the matter of my baptism is the most provoking. Neither of my parents was interested in any aspect of the Church, in fact, nobody in my father's family ever attended church that I knew of; why was I, the child of a Jewish mother, baptized Catholic? Was it to please my father's parents or to jolt my mother's? Was it a carefully deliberated decision or thoughtlessly automatic? As any discussion of this matter was consistently blocked by my mother over the years, I was free to formulate my own answer. I told myself, and eventually accepted as truth, that my parents decided a Catholic baptism would protect me from persecution. The internalization of this "truth" not only assisted me in my painful struggle for identity in later years, it also allowed me to view my parents as responsible, protective and loving.

The early years of my life felt ordinary and normal. I was a well-loved first and only child. My arrival had made us a family. Born to parents in their thirties, I was doted on, dressed up, put on exhibition, pampered, overfed and over cleaned. Faded sepia photographs attest to this. A pudgy baby, sitting in an old fashioned tin bathtub on the kitchen table, hovered over by Mommy and Daddy; Daddy's little girl, posing with him on the old stone bridge in our *Stadtpark*, dressed in our Sunday finery. I was taken for walks in the park and encouraged to play outdoors with my friends.

There was only so much time for a child in my parents' well structured life. Guided by the axiom that children should be seen and not heard, and only during certain hours of the day, I was put to sleep for two hours every afternoon, long after needing naps. Bedtime was stringently enforced and it was always too early for me. I would rather have been a part of whatever was going on.

I was strictly trained never to interrupt when adults were speaking and required, when visitors came, to shake hands and curtsy hello with a polite smile, then busy myself silently with my toys. I was the intruder, who often got in the way of the serious but secret business of adults, leaving me with a lifelong reluctance to be assertive, to interrupt or be in the way.

Chapter 2
Early Memories

Early recollections are sparse and sketchy. I cannot separate memories elicited from photographs from those actually recalled, nor the stories told by others, which have taken on the guise of memory.

I vividly remember being part of a complete family. While my father went to his job and my mother worked in the house my job was to play and be a good girl. *Mutti* (Mother) was a stern parent who had very little patience for my childish tears or excessive displays of emotion. She was the disciplinarian whose punishments were rarely physical. I remember that rare occasion after she spanked me, when I complained to my father after he returned from work in order to get his sympathy. His reply: "If Mutti hit you, you must have deserved it." Those words stung more than my mother's hands. However, when I was sick, Mutti nurtured me with devoted and extravagant care. I had many childhood illnesses: measles, mumps, chicken pox as well as frequent bouts of asthmatic bronchitis, painful ear and urinary tract infections.

When a fever was suspected, Mutti took my temperature with an underarm thermometer. I kept my fingers crossed hoping to have a fever, because I loved the taste of the little beads of homeopathic medicines she gave me to hold under my tongue. When I had chicken pox Mutti knit special mittens to keep me from scratching those itchy red bumps all over my body and smeared my polka dotted body with a bad smelling lotion. With mumps, I was allowed to come out of bed and rest on the couch, with one of Mutti's pretty scarves tied around my distorted neck and head. The measles were another matter. I was imprisoned in my dark room for what seemed like forever, because light was said to cause blindness. When I was about five or six years old I suffered from one of my frequent middle ear infections. The first sharp stabs deep in my ear occurred earlier that day. All day Mutti gave me fever medicine, and put warm oil into my ear. All day I was particularly cranky and tearful. Trying to soothe me with stories and songs she even let me cuddle in her lap. I finally managed to get to sleep. When the air raid siren went off, its shrillness tormented my aching ear. Despite my tearful refusal to cooperate, Mutti managed to get me dressed, wrapped in a warm blanket and rushed into the safety of the air raid shelter, carried there in the strong arms of my father.

My bouts of asthma lasted from early childhood until well after the war, especially during cold and damp weather. When I started coughing and gasping for air we had our drill. Mutti put several kettles of water on the stove to boil, while she fashioned a tent by draping a sheet over a high backed chair, pouring hot water and eucalyptus oil into a large pan on the floor. While I cuddled on her lap, struggling for breath, her nearness and warmth gave me comfort. We would sit in this tent for hours until my breathing eased. I would typically have no appetite after a night of wheezing and steaming, crankily spurning offers of food. Once, in desperation, Mutti presented me with a slice of golden, delicious smelling cake spread with a coating of fresh butter. How she managed to scrape these scarce ingredients together remains a mystery.

I went to nursery school where the teachers were nuns. While my memories are few they still hold an echo of safety, warmth and fun. The nuns in their black habits and white wimples seemed to glide among us, their sweet smiles and tender hands leading us in play and soothing all hurts. I remember building castles in the sandbox and riding round and round on a carousel. On rainy days, we played indoors with building blocks and doll carriages. Playing house and tending to my dolls were always my favorite activities.

Preparation for holidays was an exciting adventure. At Easter, one of the nuns dressed up as the Easter bunny holding a basket filled with colored eggs signaling that the Easter egg hunt was about to begin. We searched around indoors and out, shrieking with delight with each discovery of a colored egg, furry chicks or plaster bunny.

Advent, the four weeks before Christmas, was filled with happy anticipation, not only at nursery school, but also later on in religious school and church. The Advent calendar had a little window for each day. Behind each window was a surprise picture, which we opened with great excitement and ceremony each morning. Once a week we lit a candle on the advent wreath hanging from the ceiling. With each increase of one more candle, the excitement rose until all four were burning, then it was time to set up the crèche and decorate the tree. We were ready to gather around the tree and sing Christmas carols.

There was a Christmas tree at home too, but in our house, the feeling was different and confusing. We had presents and special foods, but never sang any songs. I sensed a sort of discomfort. Only later, could I begin to understand that it was not appropriate for Jewish people to celebrate Christmas, but we had to pretend to celebrate for the sake of safety.

When I was seven, I went to church on Sundays. My mother and father never attended church as other families did. I was the designated family member to fulfill religious obligations, never questioning why I went to church alone. I understood from a very early age that questions from me were taboo in our family.

I vaguely recollect an early vacation trip with my parents when I was about four years old. Or perhaps this is a fantasy I made up from the now fading black and white photos in our family album? We are in a big city. I am walking down a paved path through a beautiful green park holding my father's hand and with the other I clutch a small, round beaded handbag. *Papi* (Father) and I are strolling through a wonderland of trees and flowers filled with trilling birds and delicious smells. In another photograph, I am sitting on top of a large stone elk with proud antlers, doubtlessly having been lifted upon it by my father's strong arms. Another photograph pictures our family strolling through a lovely park. I feel safe and happy holding on to my parents' hands on either side. These were the days before regular air raids and bombings, when families could still engage in happy activities like vacations.

I liked to play in the garden outside our home. We had a small lawn bordered by asters in luscious shades of purple and pink, where I sat in the grass playing with my toys in the warm sunshine. Here I also practiced my first steps as a chubby toddler. Perhaps this is not a real memory; I was too young; therefore it may be imprinted by another series of photographs. In one I am holding my hands high above my head, held by my father on one side and my mother on the other, as I am taking some of my first steps. Both parents are smiling exultantly at my accomplishment. In another photo, I am toddling solo toward the outstretched hands of my father, maintaining precarious balance by holding on to my mother's pocketbook with one hand and a large ball with the other.

When I was about five or six years old we experienced a big

snowstorm. Our backyard was transformed into a white wonderland, covered with many centimeters of fluffy, white snow. My father bundled me up in warm clothing, including a red embroidered wool hat, and loaded me onto the sled, pulling me to the nearby park, where we slid down again and again what felt like a giant hill. Papi sat on the back of the sled holding me safely in front of him. I felt a delicious queasy excitement in the pit of my stomach as we coasted down at dizzying speed. When my toes were so cold that I couldn't feel them anymore, Papi pulled me home on the sled, where Mutti made us teaming cups of hot cocoa.

I was in my glory on the rare occasion when Papi would take me along with him to the corner tavern on a Sunday or a weekday after work, where he would relax over a beer with his buddies. I sat at the bar next to him on a high stool, sipping lemonade through a tall straw, listening to the low drone of men's voices without any interest in what they were saying. The sounds were like low, soothing music punctuated now and then by laughter or the clink of glasses.

There were also times when my parents relaxed at the tavern together and left me behind. I would sneak out of the house and stand on the garden gate to look at the corner tavern. Feeling hurt and lonely I waited for them to come home. I imagined the sounds and smells of the pub and wanted so much to be a part of them. The hours passed as the evening turned dark, and I waited and waited. Eventually I went sleepily back to my bed where I had been tucked in earlier by my mother.

My special friend was the walnut tree, way in the back of our yard; it held out its welcoming arms at all seasons. The tree towered above the rooftops in majestic height. Its trunk had such girth that it took many children with arms outstretched to encircle it. In early spring, its naked branches sprouted leaves of delicate green that gradually turned darker, forming a solid emerald umbrella of shade by summer. I spent many happy hours under that tree playing house with Erika, my doll friend. Here I pushed my little doll carriage back and forth in a little mother's effort to get her doll babies to take a nap.

In one corner under the walnut tree, were a number of rabbit cages housing the Dutch rabbits my father raised. They were my friends and I included them in playing house. In response to my remonstrations that they behave and be good bunnies, they responded with twitches of their flat little noses. Only I could understand their meaning.

My walnut tree had many talents. Early in the summer it seemed ablaze with tall, white candles, as it formed uncountable upright stalks of white flowers tipped with pale pink. Later in summer it transformed these into hundreds of round green balls hiding delicious, meaty walnuts in their hard brown shells. My friends loved to play with me in my backyard at this time of year, leaving later with their pockets bulging with walnuts.

Shade, candles and nuts were not the only gifts my walnut tree had for me. The most special attributes were its strong branches safely holding the ropes of my swing. If my father or mother were nearby, I would beg them to push me on my swing, feeling a delicious sensation as I flew higher and higher into the arms of my tree. Eventually I learned how to pump my legs and bend my body so I could swing up and up by myself and fly solo under the emerald canopy of my tall, strong friend.

Music was always in the air when I was young. It must have come from the radio. I never gave its source any thought, it was just always in the background. Too young to differentiate, I simply grew up on Beethoven, Bach and Mozart; on symphonies, concertos and chamber music, on opera, folksongs and Lieder. This became as much fuel for growing as did food and water. From a very early age I wanted to become an opera singer. I spent hours yodeling up and down the scales in my highest register, knowing opera singers needed a lot of practice. Mutti pleaded with me to stop shrieking, but I was not silenced for long. I did not become an opera singer, but maintained a great love for music all my life, and have spent many happy hours singing in countless choruses.

Innumerable memories revolve around food. While I recall with nostalgia the yeasty aroma of Mutti's baking and the pungent smells of her thick soups and *Sourbraten*, eating was usually an area of tension and tears, a battleground between my mother and me. My appetite was usually much smaller than my mother's ideas of what was sufficient nourishment. She would try to tweak my interest with all kinds of laboriously prepared dishes even when foods became scarcer. The moment I sat down at the table, my stomach seemed to close up. My mother would plead and I would take a morsel. Mutti would threaten that I could not go out and play until I ate something and I would take another mouthful. She would scold that I could not leave for school until I finished my bread and jam and I would tearfully stuff it down. Food was rarely a pleasure then, except when Mutti baked her wonderful cookies before Christmas or fried the traditional jelly filled donuts named *Berliner Ballen* to eat on *Sylvester* (New Year's Eve). Mutti never had to beg me to eat those.

We once were on vacation on a farm in the country. Our hosts had beautiful orchards with various fruit trees. The peaches and plums were ripe. As we children played among the trees, whose branches were drooping with ripe fruit, we would pick a peach here, a plum there and simply pop them into our mouths. They were sweet and warm from the sun and absolutely irresistible with sweet juices dribbling down our chins. Fruit has never again tasted that good.

Oma holding baby Ingrid

Learning to walk

In the park with Papi

In my garden

With my doll friend Erika

CHAPTER 3
GOING TO WORK WITH PAPI

MY FATHER HAD A VERY IMPORTANT JOB. He was a railroad worker, and went to work every day, except on Sundays, to keep the trains from crashing into each other. By the time I got up in the morning he was almost ready to go to work, dressed in the dark gray, double breasted jacket and slacks of his railroad uniform. I loved the way the buttons sparkled when he moved. He wore a lapel pin that told people how important he was. When finished polishing his black shoes until you could see your face in them, he was all ready to leave. Picking up his metal lunch box he gave Mutti a kiss goodbye, and then gave me a great big hug, big enough to last me the whole day until he came home again. I loved the scratchy feel of the woolen uniform when he hugged me that way.

Some days I was ready and dressed when he left for work; on those days I rode on the bar of his bicycle as far as the garden gate. He would get off his bicycle, bend to kiss me goodbye and ride off. Climbing up the garden gate to see him better I waved goodbye until he turned the corner. Before he went out of sight he would turn around and wave and throw me a kiss. In the evening I waited at the gate for him to come home. I could hear him whistling before I could see him come around the corner. When he came into sight I ran to meet him in great excitement. Without missing a beat Papi swung me up onto his bicycle and we arrived in our yard whistling a duet.

What stories Papi would tell us during supper. Stories of

passenger trains coming from far away places, stories of freight trains loaded with all kinds of things. And all of these trains went in the right direction, to the right location, without ever bumping into each other, because my Papi guided them from his high signal tower. I asked him to tell me how he did all that, and he would explain all about levers and green and red light signals, but it was really hard for me to imagine. I had some vague idea that Papi was a little bit like God up there in that tall tower, making sure that everything worked as it should below.

One day, when I was in the second or third grade and school was closed, Papi asked: "Would you like to come to work with me today?" "Oh boy, would I like to!" So Mutti packed me a lunch just like Papi's, only smaller, and put it into the metal lunch box. Off we went to work, with me riding on the bar of his bicycle all the way. I proudly waved to my friends, yelling: "I can't play with you; I have to go to work." We arrived at a lone, tall building, standing in the middle of a tangle of railroad tracks. Papi parked the bicycle and we climbed up many flights of stairs. There were so many stairs I was all out of breath when we finally reached the top. The whole building was one big chamber, with windows all around. It was a very bright room, but unlike any room I had ever seen.

There were panels with many kinds of buttons, handles and lights that blinked on and off. There were high tables with tall stools. On one table was a strange gadget that my father said he used to talk to other people. This turned out to be the Morse code machine. The strong smell of machine oil hovered over rows of iron levers that were almost as tall as I was. By switching these back and forth, my father would make the trains go in the right directions. "I'll show you," he said. "Sit over there on that high stool and watch. You must be very quiet and not interrupt because a train is coming, hear it? I have to switch the right lever to make it go into the station; otherwise it will crash into a train that is coming on the same track from the other direction." Solemnly, I climbed onto the stool, watching with rapt attention as my father put on a leather glove and hand on lever, waited until the just right moment. I heard the train come closer and closer until I saw it practically just in front of the tower, when suddenly Papi switched the lever with a hard pull. I actually saw the track move; just enough to make the huffing locomotive pull the rest of the train toward the station. Then a light turned green, signaling the other train that all was clear. A few minutes later, the other train came from the opposite direction, and chugged merrily and safely along its way.

Then Papi went to the Morse code machine, which had been clattering for a while and listened to it intently. He told me someone was telling him that another train would soon be coming along and would need his guidance. This puzzled me; I hadn't heard anybody talk to him. Papi laughed saying the message was sent in code. The machine sent dots and dashes that he translated into words. He patiently showed me how to work the Morse coder to send a message to somebody far away, by using the right dots and dashes. Then he tried to teach me. This was hard. You had to use the heel of your hand to press the lever down quickly to make a dot and longer to make a dash. Eventually, I learned how to press down the handle just right with the heel of my hand and how to fit the dots and dashes to some letters of the alphabet. "Dot, dot, dot; dash, dash, dash; dot, dot, dot." Papi said this was the most important code to know, this stood for SOS, which means somebody is in trouble. I spent hours practicing this, so if I ever needed to I would be able to send for help.

Finally Papi said "Time to go home." He had oiled and pulled so many levers, switched so many tracks, guided so many trains safely along and had received and sent so many Morse code messages, that he must have been very tired. But I wasn't the least bit tired. I could have spent many more hours practicing dots and dashes and watching the trains go by. But home we went with the smell of machine oil lingering in my nose, while the Morse code machine continued to clatter. We rode home together on the bicycle. Papi let me steer once or twice. As we drove through the garden gate, whistling *"Du, du liegst mir im Herzen"* (You are in my heart), Mutti stood at the front door waving us home.

Papi at Work

Chapter 4
Broken Glass

When did the air raids and bombings begin in Moers? Sometimes it seems that they were always part of my life, much like the weather. Sometimes it rained and sometimes the sun shone. Sometimes bombs fell and sometimes they did not. One night, when I was about four or five years old, marked the beginning of the reign of terror that eventually turned into nightly air raids.

Like all young children I resisted early bedtime, which was strictly enforced. My parents believed that after eight o'clock in the evening, children should be neither seen nor heard, but should be asleep in their beds. That evening, I had given my mother a very hard time, complaining: "Why do I have to go to bed? All my friends are still out playing?" But Mutti was firm: "It's late enough for you. How are you going to feel bright and cheerful tomorrow morning if you don't go to bed now?"

In spite of grumbling and complaining, I was in the bedroom at eight o'clock sharp. I could hear the laughter of other children outside. It was summer and it was still light. Those lucky kids were allowed to play, how come I wasn't? I could also hear the soft murmur of adult voices as my parents sat around the kitchen table in conversation with neighbors. Wishing to be part of the fun and visiting, I grudgingly stayed in my room, but I would not stay in bed and try to sleep when everybody else was still having fun.

I made up private games to entertain myself, secret games to play behind closed doors. I stole across to my parents' closet and with my nose followed the familiar scents of or their clothing. There was Papi's rough, grey wool suit. I dug my nose into it enjoying his scent and its delicious scratchiness. Here was Mutti's favorite dress, the blue, silky one she loved to wear on special occasions. It held the sweet lingering smell of her perfume. I stealthily slid it off the hanger and slipped into it, pretending to be grown up and going to a party. Tripping over the hem, it was long enough to fit me three times, I paraded up and down the room, admiring myself in the mirror of my mother's dressing table. Something was missing. I didn't really look grown up enough. I took off the dress and dug through my mother's drawers, where I eventually found her corset and bra; but the empty cups collapsed and made me look deformed. I quickly found the remedy in the dirty laundry hamper. Stuffing the cups with soiled socks and underwear, the little girl was transformed into a curvaceous lady with breasts. Now the silky dress looked really elegant as I added long beads with gloves and a matching handbag. I took care not to clump around too hard in Mutti's high heels. They were so big they flopped up and down as I tried to walk.

Eventually I tired of my fashion masquerade. Having admired myself sufficiently and having engaged in enough pretend party talk, I finally returned my attire to the closet, drawers and dirty laundry hamper, ready to go to sleep.

I shared my parent's bedroom. My little bed was placed perpendicular to the foot of their big one. Between my bed and the window there was a narrow aisle of about two to three feet. The window, of course, was covered with a heavy black-out shade under some filmy, white curtains. This was carefully drawn and tucked every night, so not the smallest chink of light could signal our presence to any potential air raiders. I was fast asleep dreaming of doll parties and games with friends. It was the middle of the night and my parents were also in bed. In my sleep I heard some tinkling sounds, was it bells, or maybe the tinkling of glass? Then the sound of my mother's voice, shrill and full of fear: "Ingrid, don't move!" she cried. "For God's sake, lie still!" Puzzled, but ever obedient, even though half asleep, I held very still, wanting to sit up to see what was going on. My father came over to my bed and very slowly and carefully began to turn my cover back, which strangely repeated that sweet tinkling of glass I had heard in my sleep. A bomb had exploded nearby (without the warning of an air raid siren), causing our window to implode. Glass had shattered into thousands of tiny pieces, falling directly into my bed. My quilt was covered with broken glass and slivers were in my hair and on my face. Now I understood Mutti's warning to lie still, as she carefully lifted the sharp little pieces off my face and out of my hair. I was very frightened and began to cry, which made the glass slivers stick to my skin. Miraculously I was not hurt beyond a few cuts on my face and scalp that healed in a short time leaving scars only on my mind.

My parents let me stay in their bed for the rest of the night, after my father had boarded up the broken window. None of us slept very much, wondering if more bombs would threaten us that night. I was calmed by the nearness of my parents and was comforted by the warmth of their bodies. I guiltily promised myself never again to complain about bedtime and definitely not to surreptitiously dress up in Mutti's clothing any more, pretending when I was supposed to be in bed. I was sure this would keep the bombs away. But it didn't. Air raids and bombings soon became a nightly occurrence.

CHAPTER 5
SOUNDS OF MY CHILDHOOD

NO MATTER HOW HARD I TRY I cannot hear my father's voice. I was eight years old when last I heard it, when Hitler's minions tore his sounds out of my life, but in the memory of my heart I can hear a symphony.

Cling-a-ling-a-ling rang his bicycle bell; I could hear it from around the corner, as it announced his return from work. "Papi, Papi, wait," I yelled. "Wait I'm coming!" I would run as quickly as my short legs could manage in order to meet him before he reached home. Swiftly he swept me up on to the handle bar of his bicycle and together we rode through the garden gate and down the walk beside the house, all the time "cling-a-ling-a-linging" with my little thumb on the bicycle bell underneath his big one. As we entered the house together we heard Mutti scolding (her voice has stayed in my ear) "Stop dawdling you two, supper is on the table getting cold." Time at the supper table was for adult conversation, and when adults spoke, children had to be quiet. Mutti's reproach would spoil my contentment: "Ingrid, stop pushing your food around your plate and eat it." Oh well, I had my glorious time on Papi's handlebar.

The music of my early childhood in Moers resonates in memory with happy harmonies. I remember sitting on a skirted lap; I couldn't have been much older than a toddler. Was it my mother, a doting aunt, or the Jewish grandmother I can't recall because she fled Germany for the shelter of Palestine while I was just a baby?

She sang a nursery rhyme in her soft voice, accompanied by hand motions which I tried to emulate.

While attending nursery school as a little tot, I joined in chorus with my friends in the songs taught by the nuns. I loved each and every one of them and when it was time for my favorite, a tune from Hansel and Gretel, I raised my reedy little voice to cadences heretofore unheard. In church (a few years later), the music was somber and entreating; I loved the sound of so many voices intoning the Latin chants *"Kyrie Eleison, Christe Eleison."* They felt like the warm soothing strokes of a giant hand, while I had no inkling what they meant. When on special occasions we marched in procession from the church to some destination no longer remembered, clad in white dresses with daisy wreaths crowning our heads, we sang songs accompanied by the rousing blast of horns and trumpets, which stirred me to ecstatic heights; I felt I was singing among the angels.

Sunday mornings I woke up to the radio. The rich sonorities of instruments and voices in symphony or opera were accompanied by the rhythmic 'swish-swish' of Papi's brush vigorously shining shoes to the beat of the music.

The sounds of war rumbled. The repeated whine of the siren warned us of approaching airplanes ready to discharge their cargo of bombs. The huffing and puffing of breath and the clatter of running feet resounded as we ran for safety to the bomb shelter, desperately trying to outrun the planes. The roar of planes was menacingly getting louder and louder. When we finally got to the bunker, the sound of clattering feet on steep metal steps was followed by a loud bang as the door clanged shut behind us. Soon you heard the thud of a hit followed by the bang of an explosion and then the wailing of frightened children and the soothing attempts of hushing mothers. "Please God; don't let it be my house." More thuds, explosions, wailing and praying. It seemed to last forever. Finally the roar of planes receded, as they went back for more bombs to drop to scare us to death. Then the all clear sounded, a long one-note wail, eliciting both relief and fear. Relief that it was over for now at least and fear as to what we would find when we climbed up from the bunker.

CHAPTER 6
AIR RAIDS

WHEN IN 1941 THE BOMBINGS CAME AS nightly recurrences with rhythmic regularity, we made a mad dash for shelter with equal regularity before the bombs started falling. With the first sound of the dreaded siren, I was pulled out of a deep sleep and hustled into some clothes. Still half immersed in whatever dream might have been interrupted, we would gallop to the nearby shelter, my mother and father on either side of me anxiously rushing me along. We could hear the ominous drone of planes with their destructive cargo approaching and would run even faster to reach the relative safety of the shelter.

When the air raids first began we would go into the cellar for safety, cowering between piles of coal for winter heat and a damp, musty smelling heap of potatoes. Gradually, my parents tried to make this a more comfortable haven by bringing down chairs, a thin mattress, some blankets, and food. Just as the cellar, with its narrow, steep flight of stairs dropping into a seemingly dark void, began to appear a little more friendly, it was decided that it was no longer safe enough. The bombings had become fiercer and more destructive.

Now we sought shelter in the cellar of a building at the end of the block, which had been especially reinforced to withstand greater assault. It was certified as the local shelter for the families in our neighborhood. The first time many families were already there, huddled on benches lining the supposedly safe walls. By the dim light of a candle stub, surreptitiously lit against the rules, I could see my friends with their mothers and siblings. There was no fun and play. We knew instinctively that this time and this place were different. Against the far wall sat Frau Winter. My mother and I had visited her only yesterday with a bouquet of sweet peas to admire her beautiful brand new baby. Now she cradled the baby in her arms, shielding it in the curve of her body to protect this new life from the deadly bombs. Somehow this shelter never took on the semblance of comfort that our cellar had previously provided. This was a stark and cold place, in which the collective fears of all seeking safety congealed into a sort of tangible dread filling every nook and corner.

This shelter also became obsolete by the increasing ferocity of the air raids, and a 'bigger and better' bunker was built deep underground, heavily reinforced with concrete in the yard of my school. It was much further from our home and it took longer to get to after the air raid siren had sounded. We would run as fast as our legs could move. Once I was so sure that a bomb would fall right on my head, that I wet my pants. I was too scared to even be embarrassed. Finally arriving at what became both affectionately and despisedly termed 'the monster' we entered through heavy steel doors, descended a very steep flight of stairs, and were met by the haunted eyes of many frightened faces. The bombs had already begun to fall and with each hit every heart held the same prayer: "Don't let it be my house, please. Don't let one fall on us."

The air raids were endless. At times, we spent most of the night in the shelter on makeshift pads huddled together under blankets for warmth and comfort, listening to the roar of planes and the ominous whistling of bombs just before they would hit with a thud and a loud explosion. Sleep eluded us. When babies and children were not crying, the room was filled with the sound of praying, pleading, cursing and sobbing. The men standing guard at the top of the stairs by the door would stealthily open it a crack after a bomb hit a target close by, and give us a report, such as: "It wasn't anywhere nearby;" or "The bakery was hit." While my father was standing guard at the door I felt safe, I knew he wouldn't let a bomb fall on us or on our house.

What a relief when the all clear would finally sound and we could go home and to bed, often only to be reawakened by that hated alarm, to return to the shelter for another raid. How strong my legs were getting from all that running. One night, after leaving the shelter, I saw a sight which haunts me still. The houses on the street before ours were on fire. Flames reached to the sky consuming kitchens, couches, beds and toys in the houses of friends. The front house walls were missing; you could look right into the rooms, as if you were looking into a dollhouse. In one house the toilet was hanging loose in space and the bathtub was dangerously balanced on two legs, while the other two were suspended in midair. When we reached home, we heaved a sigh of relief; it was still standing and had all its walls in place.

Our luck did not last long. During another air raid a bomb hit nearby and collapsed the inside walls and windows of our home, filling it with broken glass and rubble. I wanted to rush in and rescue my dolls and my treasured box of books, but was restrained by my stunned parents, warning me that it was unsafe. I don't remember which neighbors took us in for the night and where we slept; all I can remember is longing and sobbing for my poor dolls.

CHAPTER 7
MY FIRST DAY OF SCHOOL

IN THE SUMMER OF 1942, MY MOTHER and I were on a train headed for Karlsruhe, a city in southern Germany, which had been spared from Allied bombing raids. Our home had been destroyed. My father was sending us to Karlsruhe to stay with friends, while he repaired our home. Mutti and I waved good-bye to Papi who got smaller and smaller as the crowded train left the station. My parents' friends were warm and welcoming, but they were strangers to me, and I begged daily to go home. My mother tried to reassure me that Papi was working hard to fix our home. "As soon as it's ready we will go home." One day Mutti said, "I have to go home to help Papi fix our apartment; he needs my help." I was to stay with our friends, and to "be a good girl "until she returned.

Ironically that night, soon after my mother left, when I was feeling sad and abandoned, Karlsruhe experienced its first air raid. Terrified, without my parents to comfort me, I tried stoically but unsuccessfully not to cry in the cellar of our equally terrified hosts during their first experience of bombs raining down and listening to the nearby explosions. While we were in a cellar, my mother watched with helpless terror from her train window as the city, where she had left her only child for the sake of safety, was being heavily bombed.

That September, after Mutti had returned to Karlsruhe, it was time to start school; I was six years old. I would begin school here, so not to miss too much until we could return to Moers.

All the preparations were made. I had a new dress and apron, the requisite uniform for a little girl starting school. I also had a school satchel packed with a slate and several pieces of chalk, the writing materials used for beginners in lieu of paper and pencils. I proudly wore my satchel on my back, and from it dangled two spanking clean squares of cloth to be used as slate wipers.

Timidly I set out for school that morning, accompanied by Mutti, who tried hard to cheer me up. I was so scared to go to school in this strange place. I didn't know any of the children. Surely they would be much smarter than me. Suddenly I felt a sharp pain in the sole of my foot and let out a scream; a bee had stung me through my open sandal. I was marched into the office of the school nurse, where an ice pack was applied to my throbbing sole. Eventually I was brought to the classroom; a bee sting was no excuse for missing the first day of school. A place was found for me at a small desk next to a very tall, self-assured looking girl. Everybody was busy drawing things on their chalkboards. The teacher pointed my attention to the blackboard where she had drawn a row of bunnies with numbers underneath. She instructed me to draw first one, then two, then three bunnies, up to ten, on my chalkboard. At first timidly, and then with growing confidence I began to draw a big circle with a smaller one on top, adding a set of long ears and whiskers; one bunny, then another one, and then another. When the teacher came by to inspect my work, this kind and lovely lady said "Ingrid, you made the best bunnies in the whole class today." I went home proud and happy, totally forgetting the pain of bee sting. Some weeks later when our apartment was restored, my father came to take us home. I was transferred to the first grade in my local school, where I continued to be a model student learning to count and read. But I never drew such perfect bunnies ever again.

Beginning school

Chapter 8
Papi is drafted

Papi had never left Mutti alone in their eleven years of marriage. Now, there was also their cherished eight year old little girl. Papi sat at the kitchen table, rubbing his throbbing brow, reading the telegram for the fourth time. How could he leave them alone; their safety depended on him? He felt his presence had protected them; who knows what might befall them now. He conjured up the horrors of deportation to camps, disease, injuries and even death. He had repeatedly witnessed cattle cars stuffed with human cargo en route to who knew what horrors, in his work as railroad traffic engineer. His job had been considered essential to the war effort. This had thankfully kept him home to keep watch over his loved ones, until now. Now his trembling hand held the summons to serve in the armed forces of Hitler. In the middle of 1944 the forces of the despicable "Fuehrer" were being driven back from the Russian front, and more expendable bodies were needed to take the place of those being slaughtered daily. My father agonized for hours but could think of no way to avoid conscription without mortal consequences, not only to himself, but also to his Jewish wife and their child. He saw no other choice; he was to become part of this contemptible venture.

The morning he left he shined his shoes as he did every morning and sat at the kitchen table for his last breakfast. He took a few sips of coffee, but could not swallow a single bite of food for the knot in his throat. For my sake (I had been crying inconsolably at the thought of Papi going away), he adopted a brave smile and promised to return really soon. He pledged to send me a beautiful post card each day and made me promise to take good care of my mother until his return. He put on his coat and hat, kissed Mutti and me and turned to leave. Then he turned back to fold us both once more into his arms, pulled away and quickly walked out. We followed him to the garden gate waving until he rounded the corner and could no longer be seen.

At home, the air raid sirens now sounded night and day. They interrupted our sleep at night and our activities by day. Just as we returned to our beds or activities the despised sirens wailed again, announcing yet another air raid. Again, we would run to the bomb shelter and dash down the steep stairs into the belly of the cold, concrete vault of promised protection. The adults had black circles under their eyes and the children were cranky. Lessons were interrupted in school; it wasn't so bad if the sirens went off during arithmetic lessons but when they broke into the middle of reading an exciting story, you could hear the groans all around.

This was a very scary time. Papi was not there keeping watch at the top of the bunker steps to protect us. It had been a month since he was ordered into the army. He was far away now. During each air raid, listening to the droning roar of planes overhead, dreading the whistling that announced the bombs on their way to their targets, I was convinced that the next bomb would land on us. In my imagination I could see the flames burning and feel the choking smoke. What if some of the shrapnel we had seen on the ground were to hurl into me and make me bleed? What if Mutti was hurt? I tried to pray but wasn't sure God could hear me from the shelter so far down under the earth. Then I tried making silent bargains, promising to be good, studious, diligent and brave; promising to be a big girl and help Mutti; promising not to cry when I was scared, if only the bombs would not hurt us.

One day in June Mutti said we were going on a trip. I was very excited because I thought we were going to see Papi, but my mother explained that we were going on a farm vacation in the country by train. Apparently, as I came to understand later, certain rural areas so far free of air raids and bombings, had been identified as places of refuge for bomb-weary city dwellers. In our case, a small village named Stetten, in the province of Thueringen, was going to provide us with such a temporary retreat.

So many people were waiting on the platforms when we arrived at the railroad station; we had to squeeze in to get a little space to stand. We waited a very long time. I got so tired of standing that Mutti let me sit on one of the suitcases. Finally, a train arrived, and a mass of people pushed and shoved very hard to get on the train. Before you knew it, the train was filled and we didn't even get anywhere near it. The train was so packed that people were standing in open doors, on steps and hanging on to outside handlebars, even as the train pulled out. Weren't they scared of falling off? We had to wait some more. It seemed like hours but finally another train pulled into the station. This one also was already filled up. How could we get on? There wasn't any room. But this time Mutti also pushed and shoved really hard, propelling me in front of her. Suddenly I felt myself lifted up off the ground and catapulted through an open window into the carriage. I screamed for Mutti, who disappeared behind me in the crowd. Soon the train started to move, first slowly, then faster and faster, with me sobbing in despair. Suddenly I saw Mutti moving toward me through the crowd, slowly dragging our suitcases up the aisle. All seats were taken and the aisles were so crowded that many people had to stand all squashed together, holding each other up from falling when the train swerved. Mutti managed to make a place for me to sit on the little suitcase while she stood. Exhausted from the ordeal, I slept through much of the trip, waking up just in time to change trains.

The second train was already waiting on another track. It was a quaint old train, with an old-fashioned locomotive and two passenger cars with rows of wooden seats and a black pot-bellied stove. We had our own seats and ate the sandwiches Mutti had brought. I was very hungry.

The train stopped often and passengers gathered up their baggage to disembark. Soon it was our turn to get off. We had arrived at our destination. On the narrow platform, a carriage drawn by two oxen with short curved horns waited; it had been sent by our hosts to drive us to their farm in Stetten. Two barefoot boys were in charge, one a shy teenager called Aloise, the other a short, chubby boy about my age, named Franz. Little did I know then that Franz and I would become such good friends. We clattered along the unpaved country roads through a pretty, rural landscape of woods, grain fields and vineyards. With the sun warm on my face and the slow, rhythmic plodding of the oxen lulling me into a sense of calm, I began cautiously to look forward to our vacation.

Soon we arrived at a small village. Stettin consisted of a cluster of small, old farmhouses, barns and stables huddled together and surrounded by a stone wall. In the village center were a few small stores, a butcher, a baker and a blacksmith. There was a small schoolhouse and a pretty white church with colorfully decorated doors and windows and a pointed steeple. A public water pump stood in the center of the small market square. This was the only source of potable water for the village. Daily, the farm wives filled their huge barrels at the pump, and carried the day's supply home on their backs.

Bumping through the narrow dirt roads of the village, we passed little houses decorated with window boxes chock full of red and pink vine geraniums. At one point, we had to pull over to let a phalanx of loudly honking geese pass from the opposite direction. No room for two-way traffic. Soon we pulled through an open gate into the courtyard of the Gerhardt farm, our hosts. The gate was pulled closed behind us and we found ourselves in a small farmyard with geese, goats and chickens underfoot. The farm house was on one side, the barn and wine cellar on the second, and the stables on the third. The large gates through which we had entered completed the square that was the enclosed farmyard. I learned later that this was the typical style of village farms in Stetten. We were shown to our tiny but cozy room above the stables. From its windows, as from all others, hung a beautiful flower filled window box. Exhausted from our trip, Mutti and I fell into our shared bed and slept through a night without air raids.

While my memories of that month in Stetten are indistinct and misty, a few stand out in clear relief. In the beginning I was a little shy of these rural strangers who spoke in a pretty but hard to understand dialect. Soon I came to love the sights, sounds, tastes and smells of our retreat; the sounds of the animals at night, the pungent barn smells, watching cows being milked in the morning and listening to the milk pouring into the metal pail. One night we were awoken by some commotion in the barn. I started down the stairs to investigate and was told to go back to my room. In the morning, I saw a tiny new born calf in the stable, standing on its spindly, shaky legs next to its mother and nuzzling under her belly in search of milk.

The main crops around Stetten were wine grapes. Like their neighbors, the Gerhardts owned many acres of vineyard in the hills surrounding the village. The rhythm of their lives was defined by the seasonal tasks required for growing grapes and the making of wine. While we were there, it was time for pruning vines, apparently a critical task, which could be performed only by experienced adults. Mutti, after being shown how and where to cut the vines, became an able pruner. We children went into the vineyards too, but being too young to be trusted with pruning shears found other ways to keep ourselves occupied. Franz showed me around the hillsides. He knew where to find interesting bugs and showed me how to catch butterflies. On the edge of the vineyard grew a profusion of wildflowers. While he chased insects, I picked armloads of red poppies, blue cornflowers and white daisies. In the golden glow of sunset, we returned to the farm in the large ox-drawn cart, tired and bedecked in crowns of wildflowers.

Farm meals were served family-style at the long wooden table in the low- ceilinged kitchen. Our food at home was so severely rationed that the large round loaves of crispy brown farm bread, thickly sliced and slathered with farm fresh butter and homemade fruit preserves, made my eyes pop and my mouth water. Eggs freshly gathered from resident chickens and milk still warm from milking made breakfast a meal worthy of royalty. At lunch we ate freshly cured ham on thick brown bread.

A communal pitcher of young wine was passed around even to the children instead of water, which was scarce. Aloise teased me when I passed up the wine in lieu of a glass of delicious milk, but eventually I too took a little swallow from the pitcher as it was passed around and found the tickly taste delicious. I liked how it made my head a little fuzzy for a while.

On an excursion with Franz to the fruit orchards, we spent the afternoon filling our bellies with freshly picked plums. The fruit was still warm when I bit through the purple skin into the sweet, golden flesh of one delicious plum after another, the sticky juice running down my chin. That night I woke up with a belly ache and had to sit on the hard wooden seat of the outhouse toilet for hours, scared of spiders. It was worth it though.

Franz had taught me to climb the ladder to the second floor of the barn where the hay and straw were stored. I loved to clamber up there with my favorite book, spending hot afternoons alone breathing in the sweet smell of hay and straw, reading about princes and princesses. At other times I might sneak through the secret door in back of the barn which led into what I pretended to be my secret garden. This small kitchen garden was completely enclosed by old ivy covered walls with enough sun to produce vegetables and herbs, surrounded by small beds of cutting flowers. I especially loved the zinnias in their many hues of pink, red gold and mauve with cheerful golden centers. Strawflowers held endless fascination for me. I had never before seen these prickly blossoms in many colors that crunched in my fingers. The stems and leaves were green and supple like other flowers, but the petals were as dry as straw. I sat there stroking them, amazed that they could be fresh and vital and old and brittle at the same time. When picked they could last all winter long, and became one of my favorites, even now.

I learned to enjoy the pleasures of rural life, especially the Saturday ritual of baking bread and plum cakes. The baker's very large brick oven stood in an open courtyard in the village center. It was used on Saturdays by the wives of the village to bake their bread and cakes. Having prepared these at home, the women carried them to the oven on large, metal baking trays, waiting their turn to bake them in the community oven. A long procession of chattering women carrying trays on their heads moved along the central road in both directions, accompanied by the tantalizing aroma of yeast, vanilla and sweet plums. The *Pflaumenkuchen* (plum cakes) were spread on large round baking trays at least three feet across. To this day the smell of plums cooking immediately conjures up the magic of those Saturday processions and the wonderful taste of the Stetten plum cakes.

Stetten was another world, one where I totally forgot the anxiety and danger of air raids. Our month of rest and recuperation came to an end all too soon. It was time to go home again. With much reluctance and a few tears, we bade our farewells to the Gerhardt family who had become our friends. We would return to visit them again and again after the war, further deepening our attachment to the magic farm in the country. Now we were returning to the world of war and waiting for word from Papi at the front.

Chapter 9
Abandoned

Soon the net drew around us more tightly. Mutti learned from an informed friend that our name was coming up on the deportation list. We were to be sent to a concentration camp. Mutti first warned her sister in Lintfort, a neighboring town. Then my frightened mother appealed to her Gentile parents-in-law for help. That evening after dark, she woke me from a deep sleep. "Hurry," she whispered; "get u p and get dressed quickly, Ingrid." Thinking it was another air raid, I reacted quickly and jumped into my warm up suit, my usual attire for the bomb shelter. "No, no, not that outfit," said Mutti in a peculiarly tense and hurried manner that alarmed me. She proceeded to hand me one outfit, then another and yet another, until I was dressed in six layers of clothing in the middle of August. She would tolerate no objections or questions, saying, "Don't ask so much. We are going to Uerdingen to *Oma* (Grandma) and *Opa* (Grandpa), isn't that nice?" "In the middle of the night?" I asked myself silently. "And why do I have to wear all these clothes? I'm much too hot." In a short time we were on the *Strassenbahn* (tram) on our way to Uerdingen, on what now felt like an adventure.

My grandmother answered her doorbell with alarm, when we rang her bell at one o'clock in the morning. *"Was ist los? Warum seid ih hir in der Mitte von der Nacht?"* ("What's wrong? Why are you here in the middle of the night?") "They are after us," whispered Mutti, "can you find a place for us to hide?" Somehow, with the help of a friend, a small attic was found the next day where my mother could hide, while my grandparents took me in to hide me in their home.

What I had thought would be a nice brief visit as usual with my grandparents turned into a nine-month stay. I had no understanding of what was going on and no knowledge of where my mother was, or why I was staying alone with my grandparents.

"Where is my mother; when is she coming back? Why did she go away and leave me here?" These questions were with me every minute. While Oma and my aunts made some lame attempts at explanations, which to this eight year old girl didn't ring true; I knew somehow they were made up. For instance: "Mutti is in Berlin working for the war effort." Why would she go to Berlin to work, she had plenty of work to do at home? I could sense a lie, but why?

Then came the long black days of dense and deafening silence, my days in hiding. No radio played my beloved songs; no trumpets exclaimed their celebratory cadences. "Shshshsh, "said Oma when I hummed a little tune. "Shshsh," said *Onkel* (Uncle) Leo if I spoke above a whisper. Sounds were instruments of danger now, they could betray my presence. In the beginning I would stand with my nose pressed against the window watching for Mutti. When Oma tried to distract me with a chore or some schoolwork, I dutifully followed her injunction, but the knot of fear in my stomach never went away. The tears overflowed frequently, easily building to lonely sobs of abandonment. And it was really hard to eat the food Oma anxiously urged on me, it simply wouldn't go past the lump in my throat.

As the weeks passed, and then the months, it became apparent that Mutti wasn't coming back. I learned to hold the tears inside, and little by little began to take part in life at Oma and Opa's house in Uerdingen. I guess I began to accept that this is where I was now living; but always, no matter what I was doing, deep down I was waiting for Mutti.

Oma made "school time" for me every morning, during the hours I would normally have been in school. I had to sit at the table while she puttered around the kitchen, and under her watchful eye I would do my arithmetic, read my books, and write my lessons in a black and white notebook. When she would catch me dreamily staring into space, guessing I was longing for my mother, she would scold me to return to my schoolwork: "Ingrid, how do you expect to keep up with the other children in school, they are sitting at their desks hard at work, not staring off into space like you. Get back to your notebook now."

Sometimes in the afternoon, Opa would take me outdoors with him. We would go to his garden and pull out the weeds. Then we would harvest some carrots and a cabbage, and maybe dig up an onion and some potatoes for supper. I liked being with Opa. He was my grandfather so I knew he was old, but he was tall and strong. Opa didn't talk very much; he spoke few words when we were in the garden together, but I liked these a lot, they made me feel a little bit safe and less lonely. Opa was a good companion; you didn't have to think about hiding your sadness with him.

After the garden we would go to the back of the house where the Dutch rabbits lived in wire cages. Opa had a lot of black and white rabbits from Holland, (that's why they were called Dutch rabbits). They would eventually find their way to the dinner table. The Dutch bunnies would be sitting in their cages expectantly twitching their flat little noses, waiting for the delicious treats from the garden that we would bring them. I would wonder if the little rabbits missed their mommies in Holland, and as I fed them their green carrot tops I would murmur to them that they would soon be back with their mommies. One little rabbit became my favorite pet; he was small, with very tall ears. His black patches seemed to be painted on his white fur; I named him Spotty He had very long whiskers and was really cute when he twitched his nose. I would tenderly lift him out of his cage and hold him close. At first, he was a little shy and nervous but soon he got used to me and trusted me; he knew I wouldn't hurt him Spotty and I had long, quiet talks together. Well actually he listened and I talked. I would tell him that I was far away from my mommy, just like him, and that I was also living in something like a cage most of the time, since I couldn't go out of Oma's house, only when Opa took me. I told Spotty that I would take good care of him. I promised that nobody would make a roast out of him. They could eat the other rabbits, but never him. Spotty twitched his nose harder, as if in relief. I would sneak him an extra carrot green, and while he munched contentedly, we would dream of the day when Spotty would be back with his mommy in Holland and I with mine at home in Moers.

Food was very scare and strictly rationed; everyone was issued their own card with coupons for the few permitted items. Since I didn't have a ration card of my own. Oma shared her slim provisions with me, supplemented by the vegetables Opa and I would bring from the garden. He taught me to peel potatoes as thinly as possible so as to not waste any of them. We would have a peeling contest to see who could peel the thinnest longest peel off a potato. He always won. Oma had an infinite variety of cooking *Kartoffeln mit Kraut* (potatoes with cabbage) which we ate every day. A loaf of bread had to last the week. Only Oma was allowed to slice and distribute it. With her sharp knife she managed to cut paper thin slices to make it last. When on rare occasions a piece of meat found itself onto the table or into the soup, nobody but Oma knew how we got it, but the next day there might be a rabbit missing from Opa's cages.

Night was the worst time for missing home and my parents. I was sent to bed by eight o'clock, where I would lie with eyes wide open and cry. I shared my grandmother's bed, and before she came to bed, I would lie on the very edge leaving most of it available for her. The sheets weren't snow white and sweet smelling like ours at home; they had small red pictures on a white background and smelled like Oma's house. I could never get comfortable in this bed, and would get up dozens of times and wander around the dark room, which was filled with gloomy heavy pieces of old-fashioned furniture, the shapes of which scared me in the dark. Sometimes I would listen through the door, just to hear the sound of voices. One good thing about being alone in this room though, I could cry as much as I needed, nobody would hear and try to make me stop. One night I heard loud voiced coming from the kitchen. I carefully opened the door a crack only to overhear an argument between my Onkel Leo and my grandmother. In a loud voice and with his face all red Onkel Leo shouted: "Are you crazy? She can't stay here anymore. She is putting all of us in danger. Because of her we can all get shot." Slowly I began to understand that they were talking about me, when Oma responded: "She is ours, she stays here, and I don't ever want to hear another word about it." Frightened and confused I withdrew into the bedroom, asking myself: "What have I done? What makes me so dangerous that he is so scared of my presence here?

When the air raids and ensuing bombings increased in intensity, occurring at all hours of the day and night, my grandparents decided it was too dangerous to continue to shelter in their cellar.

Under cover of darkness, hidden under a blanket they smuggled me into the large concrete bunker at the corner, without anyone seeing me. I was installed into the top bunk of one of three sets of bunk beds. Oma instructed me in a most serious tone of voice that I was not to come out of the cell to which her family was assigned, that nobody must know that I was there, that it was very dangerous if I was seen. She gave me a potty to relieve myself on, and sneaked food into the room after she had eaten in the public dining room. I felt sought out for special punishment, but had no inkling what I was guilty of. I had in my possession a green satin ribbon, probably left over from some present ages ago. This ribbon took the place of my Erika doll, whom I had abandoned at home in Moers. It became my friend, confidant and companion. We whispered together under the covers, and at times the green ribbon dried my tears; it always understood when I was scared during the bombings, and angry at my severe confinement. The air raids and bombings would continue for days on end, and then there would be a quiet time when we went back to the house until the next burst, with me under cover of the blanket.

Many were the hours that I would sit on the old black leather couch by the kitchen table, supposedly doing my schoolwork, but I would be daydreaming about Mutti's return. I had a very clear picture of this in my mind. Mutti would suddenly come through the door with her beautiful smile, holding her arms out to me. We would rush towards each other and she would hold me soft, warm and safe, forever. The details of this picture would vary, sometimes Mutti would be wearing her brown winter coat with the cuddly fur collar, other times her pretty flowered summer cotton dress. Sometimes I would imagine I was asleep in bed and would be awakened by her in surprise; other times I would be busy helping

Oma in the kitchen when she would burst through the door. But always the daydream would end with a blissful reunion.

And so the winter of 1944/45 slowly dragged on, while I was consumed by longing and daydreams.

Last picture before hiding

On Board Ship

CHAPTER 10
REUNION

THE COLD-HEARTED WINTER WAS FINALLY OVER. OPA was taking me out to the garden again on air raid free days, first to turn over the soil and fertilize it, and then to begin the seeding and planting for this year's vegetables. The days were getting lighter and warmer, it was April of 1945. Early one morning, at the kitchen table as usual trying to do my 'schoolwork', it was more difficult to concentrate than usual. I felt hot and had a very bad earache. Oma took my temperature and pronounced that I had a high fever, and probably a middle ear infection. To my surprise she did not cajole me into continuing my school work but made up a bed for me on the old black leather couch behind the kitchen table She tucked me in comfortably, gave me some aspirin and told me to rest.

I fell into a sleep rife with vivid dreams spawned by the delirium of fever. At one point I dreamed that my mother came through the door with her arms open wide. She rushed toward me and held me warmly. Awakening, slowly I realized that this was not a dream, it was real. Mutti was really here.

Later she told us what had happened. As she had looked out of her little attic window during the just breaking dawn of that early morning, she saw soldiers dashing stealthily from house to house. She surmised these were American infantry following on the heels of the fleeing German Army. (Somehow she had been able to secretly follow news of the war on some forbidden radio transmission.) As more and more American soldiers began to fill the streets, she guessed correctly that Germany was losing the war and that these men were her liberators. Without further thought, she abandoned her attic and tried to dash across town by bicycle, with total disregard of danger, having only one goal and destination: to reach her child. She was stopped by American soldiers with a shout: "Stop! Where do you think you are going? Don't you know there is fighting going on?" She told them her story and they provided her with safe escort. Loading her bicycle into the back of a jeep, they drove her to Oma's house. They also verified that they were the occupying forces, with the German army in swift retreat. They warned that they would shortly be blowing up the local bridge over the Rhein River and all inhabitants of the area would have to be evacuated.

The blissful reunion was quickly interrupted by the emergency demands of a quick evacuation. I have only vague memories of this, and learned later that my grandparents had decided on one destination and my mother on another. Dazed from fever and excitement, I found myself on top of my mother's huge, soft eiderdown comforter, which she had tied onto the bicycle to fashion a comfortable bed for me where I could sleep off my fever. (How her precious eiderdown, originally part of her dowry, materialized at this time I will never know. It is one of many questions I never thought to ask her.) She pushed her bicycle with me enthroned cozily on top, and with various other supplies loaded on. In this manner, we joined the other evacuees moving in a long line, heading across and away from the Rhein. I alternately dozed and woke up in contented confusion, only to doze off again, rocked by the bumpy rhythm of the bicycle's movement.

At nightfall we arrived at a small village. We encamped at an old abandoned farmhouse. Other evacuees had preceded us there, and had already decided to make this their temporary home. In the central courtyard a large bonfire was blazing brightly, as if in welcome, and people were feeding it with books, papers, pictures and Nazi logos, the now despised artifacts of Hitler's regime. Although I did not understand this at the time, I later learned that this had been the home of a devout Nazi who had fled in fearful anticipation of the advancing allies. People were now throwing items out of the windows and doors into the bonfire with frenetic enthusiasm. Apparently, now that the German army was in defeated retreat, and the allies were not only winning, but would soon be occupying the land, former patriots were reversing their allegiance in fear of retaliation. They were burning all symbols, books, pictures and paraphernalia representing Hitler and Nazism.

We found a tiny available room under the eaves of the roof, and this is where Mutti and I spent the next six weeks, blissfully together again, until we were permitted to return to our home in Moers. I cannot recall the name of the little village of our stay, so have always thought of it as *Friedensdorf* (peaceful village).

My memories of Friedensdorf are of outdoors, probably as a result of my long indoor confinement. While the other children in the farmhouse frolicked outdoors in all kinds of fun and games, I kept a shy distance, even though my mother urged me to play with them, reassuring me that it was all right. I had been too thoroughly indoctrinated. I could not to go outdoors without a grandparent and especially could not speak or play with other children. My fear was only partially overcome with great trepidation and reluctance. What made it all right now? I would wonder; perhaps it was because my mother was back.

However, as days went by, I slowly started to play alongside one particular boy, who must have been a year or so older than me.

Erich was nice as he didn't make fun of me, of my shyness or my silence. He simply said: "Want to see where there are real frogs and fishes?" He seemed to know his way around and led the way with me following reluctantly. The first day I ventured with him as far as the edge of the garden behind the house, before a vague anxiety made me run back to the house and my mother. The following day Erich was back again with his invitation to outdoor adventure, and I followed him to the heart of the garden. I was beginning to enjoy my new freedom, albeit with guilt and unease. I felt I was breaking rules.

Eventually I began to relax enough to see the world around me, the big, beautiful world of the garden at the height of spring. With a kind of pleasure I felt way down in the pit of my stomach, I saw the spectacle of flowers blooming in a riot of colors; all kinds of flowers, tall showy red and yellow tulips, small and humble white daisies and yellow buttercups. There were proud blue irises with their velvety yellow throats, and lush heads of fragrant white, pink and mauve peonies. Some of the flowers were familiar from home and seemed to greet me like friends, others I had never seen before. Some had a strong pungent smell that teased my nose, others smelled sweet and inviting, and above and around all of them hovered bees and all sorts of insects.

I began to hear sounds I had missed so long; the soft buzzing of insects around my ears as I sat still in the meadow; the rustling of leaves as soft breezes blew and the sweet song of birds. They trilled and warbled as they sat in the treetops or flew from branch to branch in sweet freedom. I would sit still for long stretches just looking, smelling and listening, just taking in the outdoors which had been forbidden for so long.

Day by day I got a little braver in my outdoor ventures, each day following Erich a little further. One day I followed him to the edge of the woods behind the garden, taking in the magic of the trees clad in their fresh spring foliage in so many shades of green, I got lost trying to count them. In the distance I could hear the tantalizing murmur of a rushing brook, and while I felt pulled by its sound and secrets, the counter pull of my unease made me run back to the house, to make sure Mutti was still there.

The next day, however, I finally dared to go all the way to see where the real frogs and fishes were. I went with Erich through the woods to the edge of the lovely brook. Here we sat in its magic spell, watching the water skip merrily over small pebbles and large boulders. The brook sang many songs all at the same time as it made its way downstream, I could hear it trill and yodel, and at other times murmur quiet secrets. I wondered if there were fairies living at its bottom. As I watched dragonflies of multihued blues skim and dance across the surface, I had my answer.

But Erich was a practical boy and was interested in important things. He showed me where frogs hid and how to catch them. He also showed me swarms of pollywogs in the shallow water, and demonstrated with scientific abandon their various stages of development on their way to becoming frogs. He even caught some and put them in a jar, so we could watch them more closely as they evolved. It made me a bit queasy to put these little creatures into the captivity of a small jar, but Erich said that we would set them free again, just as soon as they turned into little frogs. Luckily, he was content to only point out the schools of little tiny baby fish without needing to capture them. These delicate little threads of creatures swam in the shallows of the brook around and around, as if in a carefully choreographed ballet. Entranced, I would watch their silent dance endlessly

It was high adventure for us to stand at the roadside in Friedensdorf and watch truck after truck drive by filled with American forces. Later, when Germany would be divided into four occupied zones, this would become part of the British zone, but now the American forces were coming in. As these soldiers passed in their huge army trucks, we would wave to them as much in welcome as in a plea for goodies. We must have been quite a sight, dozens and dozens of hungry urchins in tattered clothing lining the road. Food was almost impossible to get at that time and new clothes were but a vague memory of the distant past. These nice men would generously throw parts of their own rations to us from their truck windows as they drove by. There were cans of Spam and chocolate bars, packs of chewing gum and packages of crackers. Initially, I fared very poorly as everyone scrambled for these treasures. I was small and frail for a nine year old and afraid to compete. As an only child I hadn't had the requisite practice, but I quickly learned to become more assertive, prompted by hunger, and scramble for my share of the goods, which I proudly took home to my mother.

Mutti was pleased with the food, and happily watched me relish delicious chocolate bars. At the same time, she pined for a cup of coffee and a cigarette. I could not figure out how to procure coffee for her, but cigarettes, well that was another matter. I had seen soldiers throw out the butts of their partially smoked cigarettes from their trucks. So, along with my fellow gatherers, I would pick up them up and collect them in my pocket. When there were enough I would proudly bring them home to Mutti, and help her open them up and collect the remaining tobacco. She would then tear up strips of newspaper and deftly roll a new cigarette. I would feel six feet tall watching her light it up, inhale and give me a great big smile of pleasure. This would spur me on to repeat my hunt for butts the next day.

I loved these friendly men in their trucks who not only showered us with food and sweets, but who also made it possible for me to make my sad mother smile again. Some of these men had skin the color of coffee or chocolate, the likes of which I had never seen before. They looked so beautiful to me with their bright smiles and kind faces, (no doubt I was influenced by the sweet treasures they showered upon me.) I had encountered my first Negroes, now called African Americans, and so started my life-long fondness for their people; a positive bias developed through gifts of sweets to a starving girl.

The weeks passed and our stay in Friedensdorf came to an end. In June of 1945, we were finally allowed to return to our homes.

CHAPTER 11
RETURNING HOME

"WE'RE GOING HOME TODAY," said Mutti. "Hurry up, finish breakfast and stop dawdling." Our few bags were packed, and Mutti's bicycle was loaded with our belongings ready for the final pilgrimage back home to Moers. I was excited to be going home, eager to see my friends, play with my dolls. I also felt anxious. What would we find? Was our home still standing or had it been destroyed by bombs and fire? Was my own bed still there and my treasured books and precious dolls? Would anyone be there? Would Papi be waiting for me at home?

The trip took a long time. We walked with Mutti pushing her bicycle loaded with all our stuff. Tired and cranky I asked repeatedly: "Aren't we there yet?" After a long day of trudging along or lagging behind Mutti, we finally reached the outskirts of Moers. As we walked through the town toward our street, everything looked unfamiliar; most houses were in ruin; stones, bricks and concrete rubble littered the way. It was very hard to push through these streets. I could not recognize anything in this chaos. Confused and frightened, I started to cry. This was my hometown, but it felt like a place I had never seen before. Mutti had a strange, gloomy look on her face; she too must have been fearful about our house.

When we finally got to 39 Uerdinger Strasse, we found our building relatively undamaged. The walls and roof were intact; only one or two windows were broken and boarded up. There was something foreboding about how the house and its surrounding yard looked, showing the effects of war and neglect. There was silence instead of the noisy honking and hissing of the gaggle of local geese. What had happened to these scary but beloved watch geese? Did they get hurt by bombs or did they become somebody's dinner, like the Dutch bunnies? The yard was overgrown with waist high weeds. Broken concrete pipes and gravestones (which had previously been manufactured here) were scattered helter skelter all over. These had always before been stacked in neat, orderly rows.

We walked slowly up the tall flight of stairs to our apartment fearful of what we would find. To our surprise the apartment seemed undamaged, but it was completely empty. Where did our furniture go? What happened to everything? Where were our couch, table and chairs? Where did my little bed go? Our furniture and belongings had been removed to and stored in one of the concrete factory storerooms. Was that done to safeguard our things, or did someone need to hide all evidence of our ever having lived there? Was our furniture hidden to keep it safe just like Oma and Opa had kept me hidden in their house to keep me safe?

We hunted for our belongings in the storeroom, which was in total chaos; so much stuff it was hard to find anything. Soon Mutti found the dining table under some dirty covers, then the chairs and breakfront. She started to cry when she saw that it was in good condition, only marred by some water stains. There had been a fire in the storeroom but the only damage to our things was water damage. After all we had been through, a few water stains on our dining room furniture and water-logged books and toys mattered little. Suddenly I found a sad and soggy box with my best treasures. "Look, here are my books!" I shouted happily. The Grimm fairy tales were here, but Sleeping Beauty had a big, ugly stain on her face from the water. The pictures had come loose in my nature collection. It didn't matter, I could paste them back in.

The search continued and we found most of our possessions, but where were my dolls? What had happened to my babies when I left them behind? My search became more frantic, when in a dark corner I spotted a familiar head. "Hansi, here you are, my baby boy; mommy is here," I cried as I retrieved my favorite boy doll. Close by was my little baby doll, naked and cold, with its blanket crumpled up near by. I cradled it, my tears washing its pathetic little body. I could not find Erika though, my very favorite girl doll; she had always been my make believe sister. "Erika," I shouted, as if the doll could hear me and answer back. "Erika, where are you; I'm back! Come out, come out wherever you are." When Erika did not appear I cried for her and for everything; for the sadness when Mutti left me, for the war, for my father who had not been waiting for me at home. Then Mutti shouted excitedly: "Ingrid, quick, look what I found." She had found Erika. My poor doll had been jammed between some pots and pans, soiled and dusty. I gently lifted her from the debris and lovingly cradled her. Then I saw that my poor Erika had sustained a grave injury; her celluloid head was cracked from neck to crown. I gathered my little doll family and brought them back into my room, where I cleaned them with great care and put them into a box fixed up as their new bed. Erika was given a special bed all her own where she could recover from her injury. Mutti helped me clean and dress her wound with a soft plaster and knitted a pretty hat for her, which covered and protected her injury. It was so good to have my little sister back again. I could again whisper secrets and wishes into her ear; she was always such a good listener.

For the next several weeks, I helped Mutti put our home back together. I worked as hard as I could with this difficult job, otherwise my mother would have carried, moved, lifted and emptied big, heavy cartons all by herself. My father had not come home yet. I was driven by the fantasy that the quicker we made our house pretty and comfortable again, the sooner Papi would be home.

During this time there were a lot of ominous sounding whispers among the adults, and whenever I would come within earshot they stopped. I heard words like "deported" and "concentration camps"; I had no understanding that they were mourning the death and disappearance of friends and relatives who had been sent to Hitler's concentration camps and burned in gas ovens. While I did not understand what they were talking about, I heard just enough to terrify me, filling in with imagination what my mother would not explain.

Too frightened to let my mother far out of my sight lest she disappear again, I begged to be allowed to sleep in my father's bed. It was right next to hers. I could not see my mother and keep watch over her from my own bed. I began to have terrifying nightmares about dark and scary places that threatened to swallow me up. I dreamed about being lost and forever searching. My mother tells about the time I walked in my sleep. One time I walked into the kitchen, still sleeping, draped in several layers of her clothing, urgently warning her that we had to leave before something vague but ominous would happen. I also became morbidly afraid of thunder, which reminded me of exploding bombs.

Even more frightening was the story of how our landlady, Frau Meyer, had evaded persecution. Her husband, the concrete factory owner, had built an underground shelter for her by sinking one of the big concrete pipes six feet under the ground. This is where she lived for nine months. A smaller pipe served as an air vent and as a conduit for food. It was said that she descended into this concrete grave with a full head of red tresses, and climbed back out half her previous size with snow white hair. The sight of white-haired Frau Meyer sent scary chills down my spine. She reminded me of the scary witches in my now water-stained fairy tale books.

It had taken several weeks of hard work, but Mutti and I, having spent long hours of every day scrubbing, cleaning, polishing, unpacking and putting everything in its place got our apartment all fixed up. The beds were all made. The curtains were washed, starched and mended, and took the place of the previous ugly black out shades. Our clothes had been freshly washed, ironed and were folded and put into their drawers and closets, including Papi's. He had not come home yet, nor had we heard from him. So I began my daily vigil. Every day, sometimes two or three times a day, I walked to the railroad station and watched incoming trains discharge their passengers, convinced that my father would soon be one of them. I wanted to be the first one there to welcome him. Day after day, week after week and train after train I waited. I did not lose faith always believing he would soon be back. But what was taking him so long? Mutti tried to stop my trips to the train station at first gently, then with greater firmness, then with signs of anger. She tried to tell me that maybe Papi would not be coming home on a train, and that he might not be coming home again at all. I could not hear this. I would not believe that Papi was dead and would never come home again. He had promised he would come home to me.

Later in life as an adult, when I had grown up and had little girls of my own, I finally believed my father would never be coming back. I would think about him and how he died. Had he known how scared I was during air raids without him to protect me? Did he know that when I was in hiding, his mother and father protected and loved me and kept me safe from the Nazis? I wondered how it had been for him. How he must have hated fighting in an army for which he had contempt. Had he been a brave soldier or was he also frightened at times? What were his last thoughts before he was killed? Was he terrified when the partisans stole over the hill intent on killing? Or was he asleep and spared awareness of what was happening? Did he think about Mutti and me? I believed that he thought of us in love, and was comforted.

CHAPTER 12
EARLY DAYS AT HOME

MEANWHILE THOSE OF US WHO HAD RETURNED were trying to begin to live some kind of life again. It was really hard because nothing was the same anymore. What had not been destroyed in our town by bombs or fire was rendered hazardous by water damage and the effects of looting. Wherever we went we saw grotesque and charred ruins where formerly there had been familiar houses and buildings. We got lost in streets we had walked all our lives. They had become unrecognizable. The house next door had sustained a direct hit. The entire front was gone, leaving bare the open rooms for all to see the evidence of ruined lives within. When I found my school in ruins, I was inconsolable. I had been dreaming of going back to school again with my friends for such a long time and now there was no school. It took many months before the schools were sufficiently repaired so that classes could be held.

We had survived the hardship of hiding and hunger, of bombs, loneliness and anxiety, but it had taken its toll on body and spirit. Mutti had become so thin you could practically see through her, and her beautiful thick, black hair had turned into thin strings of dreary gray. She coughed all the time and there was something in her eyes that scared me. I missed the way her eyes used to sparkle when she smiled. I missed the softness of her arms when she hugged me. She didn't smile at all anymore and sharp words had replaced loving ones. I was in desperate need of comforting, consumed by fears and anxiety night and day. By night, I had nightmares and walked in my sleep; by day, I was frightened by loud sounds. A clap of thunder propelled me to the bathroom with a sudden attack of diarrhea. What terrified me most was any separation from my mother no matter how brief. When she was out of my sight I would shake with fear, convinced that this time she would not come back. Poor Mutti, she could barely go to the bathroom without me clinging to her. When she went to one of her many doctor and dentist appointments, Mutti asked Frau Meyer to watch me. This scary neighbor had little patience for a frightened "mommy's baby" and would angrily admonish me to grow up and behave. The next time Mutti had to go to the dentist, I begged her to let me stay home by myself, where I could cry in comfort and anxiously watch for her at the window.

There were endless visits to the dentist. The effects of hiding and lack of proper nutrition had caused her teeth to come loose and many of them needed to be extracted. One day after she came home from her ordeal at the dentist, her top teeth had been pulled. Her mouth looked strange, scarily hollow and she was in terrible pain. I was desperate to make her feel better and anxiously searched for the familiarity of her face, which had apparently been removed by the dentist, but Mutti in pain needed to be left to suffer by herself.

My own health had also been undermined by malnutrition. I had no appetite and was losing weight daily. Doctors decided what I needed to perk up my appetite were ultraviolet treatments. So thrice weekly I crossed the street to St. Joseph's Hospital where nurses, nuns in black habits and white wimples, administered the treatment. At first I was nervous; after all I was in a hospital. When these kind ladies gently explained what was to happen, my earlier experience with nuns soothed me. I was led into a room with a bed draped in white linen, above which hung an ominous looking contraption. I was given dark goggles: "Can't expose your eyes to the rays; they could make you blind," explained the kindly nun. I climbed onto the bed and lay down on my back, nervously awaiting the supposedly healing rays. My fear was growing as my memory went to the fearsome gas masks we had been forced to wear at the beginning of the war. Those ghostly looking rubber contraptions with the long air hoses had scared me to death. Soon I began to see a blue haze and feel a soothing heat on my face from the ultraviolet lamp. The treatment lasted only a few minutes and I was allowed to remove the goggles, climb off the table and go home. Did the months of treatment perk up my appetite? I can't say that it did. To this day, whenever I smell the particular odor of ultraviolet, I am reminded of St. Joseph's Hospital, where, incidentally, I had also been born.

Food was very scarce, but Mutti's sheer determination and creative energy kept us from starving. The stores that were still standing were bare of merchandise, but slowly some items began to appear on their shelves. The milkman came once or twice a week with huge milk cans on a horse drawn wagon, ringing his bell to announce his arrival. All the women would rush out with jars or pitchers to have them filled with a thin, watery, slightly bluish fluid called milk, which helped nourish us for the next several days. The precious liquid was stored in a small icebox without ice; which was impossible to come by. The bakery had been destroyed by bombs and now consisted only of a small room with a couple of tables. When the baker was able to bake a few loaves of bread once or twice a week word spread quickly. In no time the line of waiting women stretched down the block and around the corner. Often when Mutti got there, the tables were empty, the bread gone.

On occasion the butcher received a rare side of horse meat or a few rabbits and the lines would form faster than you could say 'meatloaf'. It was hard to comprehend how the underground grapevine operated with such speed. I would often go with Mutti because once the butcher had given me a delicious slice of bologna. As the line slowly snaked closer to the precious possibility of a real meat dinner, my head was filled with dreams of bologna. Would the butcher reward me with a slice today?

The times that elicited the most excited hopes and fantasies of delicious possibilities were the days my mother got on her bicycle to ride into the country to barter with the farmers. She took clothing she had knitted with yarns recycled from older knitted garments. In return for a pair of long underwear for a farmer, or a sweater to keep the wife or daughter warm, my mother would receive a cabbage, some potatoes, a few carrots or apples when in season. Best of all were the rare occasions when she brought home a bit of butter or a precious couple of eggs. I waited eagerly to inspect her basket. If there was butter and an egg, I knew she would bake a cake. Mutti was the best baker in the whole world and could produce a miracle of a cake from the most minimal ingredients.

Once she came back from her round of farm visits her bicycle basket was filled with fresh produce. There was also a brown paper bag that seemed to move. Seeing me look at it Mutti said: "Why don't you look inside?" To my surprise there was a tiny kitten in it.. I gently lifted it out and cuddled it to my chest. It was black with a white splotch on her chest and four white paws. I decided to call it 'Bootsie'. This was the most delicious surprise Mutti ever brought home.

CHAPTER 13
NO TEARS JUST FRIED POTATOES

"I HAVE TO GO ON A TRIP today," said Mutti one early morning several weeks after we had returned home. "I will be home by evening. You will stay with Frau Meyer, please be good and don't give her any trouble." I had learned asking questions never brought any real answers these days. There was also something especially closed and somber about Mutti's expression this morning, warning me not to ask why, where or what. Although I was very apprehensive about where Mutti might so suddenly need to go, I sensed that this mysterious trip had something to do with the hushed whispers I had been overhearing lately. I felt scared wondering if something terrible had happened to Papi, it was taking much too long for him to come home.

The prospect of staying with the white haired Frau Meyer was even scarier than staying home alone. I screwed up my courage and managed to convince Mutti that I was old enough to be home by myself. I was a big girl now. I had turned nine recently, on June 6, 1945. I promised to be very good and not cry while she was away, so Mutti agreed.

The day stretched endlessly, but I was determined to be very grown up and keep my promise. I decided to play school to help pass the time; my dolls would be the pupils. I propped my old school slate up on a chair, imbuing it with the status of 'blackboard', and lined up my dolls facing it. Hansi and Erika sat in the front row, with baby doll and the rest of the motley crew in the back. I taught them their letters and numbers and frequently had to chide them for inattention or misbehavior. Being the teacher helped my courage, teachers have to be stern. Mutti had left me some black bread and jam for lunch, which I shared with my doll students during 'recess'; then lessons resumed. Both pupils and teacher eventually tired of the game and school was pronounced closed. Then I crawled on the couch under a warm, woolly blanket for a rest, holding Erika in my arms. "Don't worry," I whispered in her ear, "Mutti is only gone for the day; pretty soon she'll come home and we'll have supper, and everything will be fine." But Erika wasn't so easily soothed; she had more worries on her mind. She was thinking about those scary whispers among the grown ups during the last few evenings. Hadn't she overheard them talk about soldiers in the army being killed? Our courage began to desert us and Erika and I began to cry under the blanket very quietly. Did this trip have something to do with Papi? Did Mutti go somewhere to find out about where he was and why he hadn't come home yet?

Screwing up my last shreds of courage I decided to get up and clean the house. Surely if I scrubbed and polished the house the way Mutti liked, she would come home with good news tonight. So I dusted, swept and polished the rooms until everything shone. It was almost six o'clock and it couldn't be very long till Mutti would come home. I opened a window and leaned out to catch a glimpse of her as soon as the turned the corner. I waited for thirty minutes, I waited for an hour and I still waited longer. The sun was beginning to set; soon it would be dark. Where was Mutti? What was keeping her so long? My heart beat anxiously, and I could no longer hold back the tears of fear, even as I valiantly tried to remind myself that she had said she would be back this evening. I was so hungry my stomach was growling, but I could not leave the window to fix myself something to eat.

Hours went by, the evening was dark now, and it was hard to see anything in the street. The streetlights were still broken from the war. Somehow I must have fallen asleep with my face on the windowsill, because it was in that position that I heard the door open and Mutti walk in. I must have been a bit disoriented, because it seemed that she was coming back to me from hiding; but no, that was some weeks ago and she was back now from her day's errand.

I ran to her, relieved and happy that she was back, but stopped short from running into her arms halted by the expression on her face. She looked very pale and drawn and something in her swollen eyes frightened me. I knew better than to ask questions and quietly waited. Mutti only said: "Have you had supper?" I answered: "No, I was waiting for you." "Well, go and peal some potatoes," she ordered sternly. We will have some fried potatoes." Obediently I pealed the potatoes, which Mutti efficiently fried with onions, but we couldn't swallow a single bite.

Thus, we wordlessly mourned my father's death that evening. My mother had been to visit the only survivor of my father's platoon, when they were overcome by resistance fighters. This man testified to the fact that now could no longer be denied. My father had been killed.

Chapter 14
Packages from America

COMMUNICATION WAS SLOWLY REESTABLISHED IN THIS WAR-DESTROYED country. Families all over the world began searching for loved ones in the prayerful hope that they had survived the slaughter. My Uncle Erich, my mother's brother who had safely left Germany in 1938 and settled in Worcester, Massachusetts, began to seek us via the various Jewish organizations. They discovered we were alive and living at our old address. How my mother wept when her brother's first letter arrived with thankful praise for our survival and anxious questions about our welfare. Soon letters started crossing the Atlantic Ocean back and forth between Worcester, Massachusetts and Moers *am* Rhein, West Germany, with details of our experiences, our pain over my father's death and the most immediate anxiety, how to get enough to eat during this hungry, barren postwar time.

By the grace of my dear aunt and uncle, we began to receive packages from America, for which we were envied by our equally starving friends and neighbors. The first packages contained basic survival stuff such as flour, sugar, rice and cereal grains. Soon, they began to contain such unheard of wonders as cocoa and packages of pudding mix. The letters went back and forth, in one direction asking us what else we needed, and in the other thanking our angels of mercy and making modest requests. They were followed with more packages of wonders. I especially recall the time my mother ecstatically received cigarettes and real coffee, and I was showered with chocolate bars and chewing gum. These were undreamed of luxuries which we savored and hoarded to last as long as possible.

There was one package that was truly a dream. A yellow slip of paper was delivered at home announcing a package for me. Yes, it had my name on it and was just for me, and it was waiting at the customs office. I could barely contain my eager excitement as I begged Mutti to drop everything and rush downtown to get it. When we arrived at the customs office, a long line of people were ahead of us. Hopping from one foot to the other as I impatiently waited our turn. I must have gone to the bathroom at least three times. Finally it was our turn. The man asked what we wanted and I, generally a quiet and decorous little girl, yelled out; "We want our package from America." But this bureaucrat wasn't the least bit influenced by my eagerness and excitement, nor inclined to skip unnecessary steps. First he requested the yellow slip then my mother had to fill out more papers. He went into the back room and stayed there for what felt like ages. Finally he came out with my package in his hands. He insisted that we unwrap it in his presence and remove its content for him to inspect for customs dues. The nerve, this was my package with my things in it and he insisted on snooping and staring. What did he think Aunt Ruth had sent me, bombs and bullets? It was necessary for Mutti to pay custom duty on various items, and at last we were free to repack and take my treasures home.

Safely home, I slowly and with bated breath lifted out my gifts one by one. First removing the packaging material, I lifted out a box of cocoa, enough for many months. There were marshmallows and a package of Oreo cookies. There was more chewing gum, that strangely sweet and wonderful substance that you never swallowed and which could stay in your mouth for hours. There was a lovely little book about a puppy. Folded inside was a small handkerchief with a picture of the same puppy. I swore never to use it to wipe my nose; it would always stay new and pretty. Next, I lifted out something blue and gauzy. Were my eyes deceiving me or was this really a beautiful brand new light blue dress with white eyelet trim on the collar and pockets? New clothes were not available in Germany yet. How my friends would admire me when I wore it, on special occasions only, of course. There was one more item at the bottom of the box wrapped in many layers of paper. I eagerly tore off the wrapping and from its cocoon of tissue paper emerged the object of my deepest desire. How did Aunt Ruth know what I had been wishing for ever since my treasured ball had disappeared after our house was bombed. New balls were unavailable during the war; all rubber had been used for the war effort. This ball from America was so beautiful; brand new, shiny, big and round, measuring at least ten inches in diameter. It had blue and red stars on a background of white, I had never seen anything so gorgeous. I bounced it to test it out, and squealed for joy; never had a ball bounced so high.

During this anxiety-ridden postwar time, when we strove and struggled to reestablish some semblance of normal life, it was letters from relatives and their thoughtful packages that softened the severity and eased hunger. Especially the one with the marshmallows and cookies, the dress and the red, white and blue ball.

CHAPTER 15
BACK TO SOME NORMALCY

IT WAS 1946, THINGS WERE VERY SLOWLY returning to something resembling normalcy. The rubble in the streets was cleaned up and private houses and public buildings were undergoing a slow process of repair. Electricity was available now for more hours of the day as was potable running water. More groceries appeared on the shelves and the streetcars were running. School buildings had undergone sufficient cleanup and repair to allow some classes to be held. The church had been cleaned up, its windows repaired, albeit with clear glass where previously there had been beautiful stained glass. The nightmarish memories of the war were softening and our home life slowly acquired a less anxiety-fraught routine, although the pain of losing Papi was still sharp.

My classmates and I were now able to return to school if only for part of the day. Upon entering school in the morning, we were met with the aroma of cooked cereal prepared for us hungry children in huge vats. The hot gruel was delicious and got our day off to a good start. It was lovely to greet former classmates but everybody looked different. All my friends were taller, thinner and older and all, including me, were dressed in shabby looking clothes. I felt a reluctant shyness with these familiar but strange girls and boys. When lessons started I was in my glory again; I had always thrived on the disciplined atmosphere of learning. My favorite subject was English , but I hated gym.

All my friends were riding their bicycles for fun while I ran behind them. They had all learned to ride earlier, while I was busy trying to survive in hiding. Now I wanted to learn how to ride too, but there were no bicycles to be had. Mutti must have also thought that it was high time for me to know how to ride. True to her resourcefulness, she somehow managed to collect old bicycle parts, a wheel from here, a steering handle from there, until she collected enough parts to have a bicycle built for me.. Now I had to learn to ride it. My friends took turns teaching me, running after me holding on to the saddle as I made my first shaky attempts. I fell often, but determinedly picked myself up, brushed myself off and started all over again. One day I found myself riding at a good clip and when I turned around I saw that I was riding all alone with nobody holding on. Thrilled, I rode around the block, but had not learned how to stop. I just let myself fall with the bicycle sustaining another bleeding knee. I eventually learned how to use the brake to halt the bicycle and now nothing could stop me. This was the beginning of a series of lovely adventures with my friends, as our horizons expanded with the distances that could now be covered. One day we were riding near St Joseph's Hospital, when a man came out of the bushes, calling for our attention as he exposed himself. Screeching and laughing, my friends and I rode quickly on. Only after we had put safe distance between the flasher and ourselves, did we stop to excitedly chatter and anxiously giggle about what we had seen. After this we changed our route, avoiding St. Joseph Way.

On Sundays, I began going to church again. I belonged to a church-related girls group where teaching and instilling Catholic doctrine was the main focus. While we participated in weekly teaching sessions led by the priest, I mostly cherished the fun and the friendship. We took trips together wandering the countryside and staying the night at youth hostels. We were forever singing. Sounds of songs in girlish harmonies rivaled the songs of the birds. We sang when we were in the parish house or wandering in the countryside. We sang when we were lodged overnight. We sang when we were full of energy in the morning and we sang when we were tired in the evening. No matter what the mood, we sang the beautiful Lieder of my girlhood.

On the contrary, my mother alone now without a mate, was wretched. She was determined to leave this place that caused her so much suffering and heartache.

She had begun to make arrangements to immigrate to America. My Uncle Erich in Worcester had agreed to sponsor us so we would be allowed to immigrate there. This would be a complicated, bureaucratic process and would take a long time. I was very upset with Mutti's plans and did not want to leave my familiar home, my friends and school. I had not really accepted that my father would never return, and worried how he would find me, living in America and speaking a strange language.

In our church group it was the custom for older girls to mentor the younger ones on a buddy basis. Erna who adopted me in this fashion decided to ensure my proper Catholic learning and behavior. I had a crush on her the way young girls sometimes do. She was five years older than me, sixteen to my eleven. My goal in life was to be just like her. She seemed wise and sophisticated and was everything I could ever hope to be. Having heard of the likelihood of my immigrating to America in the near future, she sought to secure the safety of my soul in my new environment. Reminding me that Christianity developed out of Judaism many hundreds of years ago, and that Christ died on the cross for me too, she warned: "Ingrid, your relatives in America are Jews, they may try to persuade you to become Jewish too. Remember that if you do this, it will be like going backwards." Puzzled and confused at this revelation, I nevertheless assured her and myself with: "I would never do that; don't worry Erna. I will always be a good Catholic. I wouldn't know how to be anything else."

In anticipation of our move, my mother hired a tutor to teach me English, deciding that, since children learn a new language more readily than adults, I would become her mouthpiece. Two years later, as the impending trip was to happen shortly, Mutti liquidated our apartment and we temporarily moved in with *Tante* (Aunt) Trude, my mother's sister, who had returned from her ordeal in a concentration camp a few years earlier. There I overheard snatches of adult conversation, which hinted that somehow being Jewish and having been deported to the camps were related. Afraid to bother Mutti with my questions, I began to have some dark suspicions and fears, but dutifully suppressed them and concentrated on matters at hand. The reality of the impending move to a new country was becoming very real and frightening.

CHAPTER 16
DIFFICULT CHOICES

"IT'S TIME TO BEGIN PACKING," MUTTI ANNOUNCED one day in the spring of 1949. We will be leaving for America soon."

Now I was forced to face what I had been avoiding for as long as possible. I did not want to get ready to leave for America. I did not want to leave at all. At thirteen years old I did not want to leave my friends, my school, my home, and everything that was familiar, to go to a strange country. I still had no understanding that our hiding and suffering had been the result of Hitler's persecution of the Jews. All I knew was that Mutti and I were reunited (although Papi had not come back). It was good to be back home again leading what felt like a regular life. My mother was definitely determined to leave as soon as possible. She had managed to acquire a visa for the United States where her brother would be our guarantor. Our number on the quota list was moving up and soon we would have to leave for a short stay in a displaced person's camp in preparation for our immigration. It was time to pack our belongings. In spite of my pleading, I was forced to decide what to take.

Two large, heavy-duty, green duffel bags filled with our belongings would be shipped ahead to our destination. So began the need to make difficult choices, what to take and what to leave behind. Of course, I wanted to take all of my dolls, which even at thirteen, were still so very important to me. Mutti said that there would only be room for one doll, and that I had to decide which one. "How can I leave my babies behind," I cried. "If I can't take my dolls, I have to stay here too. My dolls need me."

I did finally have to make my selection. I chose to take Erika, whose head was injured during the war, and whom I had lovingly nursed back to health. She and I could not get along without each other; she was my friend, my sister, my confidante. She held all my deepest secrets in her celluloid heart. I carefully wrapped her in a blanket and lots of paper to protect her. Gently placing her into the darkness of the deep duffel bag I assured her that she would be safe and we would soon be together again.

Next came my treasured books. These would of course have to go to America with me. But Mutti had other ideas saying "they are too heavy and take up too much room;" after all, our packing space was limited. I held back my tears and valiantly tried to convince Mutti with the logical argument that I would need to continue to be educated and literate in America, wouldn't I. These were the best children's books in the world, after all, she had given me most of them herself. Mutti remained unmoved by my arguments. The tears that followed didn't convince her either. So I lovingly put my Grimm's fairy tales and my beloved mythology books back into their box and slid it under my bed, knowing I had only a brief time left in which to read them one last time.

"Of course, you will want to take your accordion, Ingrid," pronounced Mutti. "It will take a lot of precious space, but it's important. You have been working so hard at your lessons and are beginning to play so beautifully. It will be good for you to be able to continue playing in America."

This was actually the last object in the world I wanted to take. I hated the sound of the accordion. I hated to play it, pushing and pulling at this bulky squeeze box hanging heavily from my shoulders and pushing on my chest. I didn't have the heart to say this to my mother who had chosen this instrument for me in such a unique and loving manner. Some months earlier I had pleaded with her to get a piano. "Please, can't we get a piano," I begged. "I love the way a piano sounds. I want to learn to make beautiful piano music. I promise I will practice every day. Please Mutti, can we?"

My mother was visibly moved by my pleas, but gently explained that we could not get a piano because we would be moving to America soon. She did however make arrangements for piano lessons. The teacher lived across the street from us and I was to use her piano for one hour a day for practice and go there for my weekly lessons. I was initially delighted with this, but it was short-lived. When I sat at the piano, hammering away at the strange keys and making many mistakes, I became aware of the presence of my teacher in the next room. This inhibited my ability to relax and practice. I imagined that she heard every mistake and judged me unfit. I stopped taking piano lessons after three short weeks, which to me seemed eternal.

Undaunted, my mother found a creative solution She bought an accordion, which after all did have keys on one side just like a piano, and was much more portable. I never dared tell her that it didn't sound the least little bit like a piano and that I hated its sounds. Dutifully I took weekly lessons at the local music school and practiced in the privacy of my home every day. In spite of my distaste for the instrument, I learned to play fairly well. So, my accordion was shipped to America.

CHAPTER 17
THE VOYAGE

THE DAY FOR OUR DEPARTURE HAD FINALLY come. We had been preparing for our move to the United States for what seemed forever. I had received private tutoring in English for several months and my teacher had told me I was ready to converse in the language of the new country. Well, I wasn't so sure, but I would have no choice, since my mother had decided that I would be the English speaking spokesperson for the family when we arrived. Besides tutoring I had also received a head start in school where we had been learning French and English.

Our household had been liquidated. The countless difficult decisions and choices had been agonized over and made. The furniture had been sold or given away, as had all those belongings that we could not take with us. We had spent the last several weeks in Kamp-Lindfordt living with my mother's sister, Tante Trude. I had been commuting daily from there to go to school in Moers. Our suitcases were packed and all those sad goodbyes had been said. My friends and schoolmates had given me pictures and small keepsakes and the memory of our tearful farewell hugs still lingered in my body.

On the morning of our departure we rose while it was still pitch dark. That was no problem for me; I had been sleepless all night. Mutti and I dressed in our traveling clothes and hastily ate a small breakfast. "You can't take such a long trip on an empty stomach," Tante Trude admonished. I painfully forced down a half a slice of bread and jam. Mutti could only manage a cup of coffee and a cigarette. I guessed she must have been sad and nervous too. I really can't remember how we got from Kamp-Lindfort to the train station in Moers. I must have been in a daze because suddenly we were at the train station. The whole town seemed to be there to see us off. The entire station house was filled with friends and family members, even Oma, Opa and Onkel Leo had come. So the hugging and the goodbyes had to be suffered again. Try as I would, it was impossible not to start sobbing as aunts and uncles, cousins and neighbors, schoolmates and best friends pushed their way to hug and kiss me goodbye once more. Finally, the train pulled into the station. I was lifted up onto the high steps of the train's passenger car; and Mutti followed. Our luggage was handed up and stored on the overhead rack. I sat down near the window with Mutti next to me. As the conductor called "all aboard" and the train started to move, Mutti and I leaned out the window for one last wave. There was Opa waving his white handkerchief like a flag, with Oma holding hers over her face. There was Onkel Leo waving stiffly goodbye, and there were Sigrid, Kristel, Maria and all of my friends and schoolmates, waving and singing: "*Must du denn, must du denn, must du wieder, wieder gehn?*" – (Must you really go away?) We waved and waved as they got smaller and smaller until we could see them no more.

We traveled for many hours finally arriving in Hamburg, worn out and exhausted from crying. I had slept most of the way. We were met by official looking people who escorted us to a bus and were driven to a camp for displaced persons, to be "processed" for immigration. Mutti had to stand in line daily to complete dozens of forms and questionnaires. Here we were also deloused, examined and poked, injected and sprayed and finally declared sufficiently healthy to leave. After six weeks when the needed paperwork, inoculations and health exams were finished, we were ready to embark on our sea voyage to America. A train took us to the harbor in Bremerhafen.

Carrying only our hand luggage, (the rest had been loaded on board earlier), we stood in a long line of passengers inside a kind of debarkation shed. The line moved forward very slowly, but finally we came out of the shed. There, in a very narrow canal of water stood a gigantic ship with a gangplank connecting it to the concrete on which we stood. I was puzzled and disappointed. How could this huge ship move in its narrow confines and get us to America. I had never before seen the ocean, and had imagined it as huge, deep and full of waves. How could this be the North Sea? There must be some mistake. I did not know that this was only a berth for the ship to anchor and that the real ocean was beyond the harbor.

The line moved forward and soon it was our turn to climb up the gangplank. We were given a card with directions to our accommodations. I followed my mother as we walked down several steep metal stairways, along long narrow hallways, down some more steps, then some more, and finally we found ourselves at our designated quarters. This was a large room with eight sets of bunks. We claimed one bunk, which was in fact two hammocks, one hanging two or three feet above the other. Mutti took the bottom one and I was assigned the top. Soon other passengers arrived and claimed their beds among shouts of confusion. They were speaking in a language I had never heard, a language that sounded familiar and unfamiliar at the same time. It sounded to me like German, but wrong. Mutti explained that they spoke Yiddish, the language spoken by Jewish people from Eastern Europe. Much later I came to understand that these were the survivors of the Holocaust from Poland. These were the real displaced persons, for whom the refugee camps had been their only home since the war.

As the journey progressed I came to know some of them very well. Malka, who was traveling to America with her mother and stepfather, and I became good friends. We spent many hours entertaining and distracting each other during this difficult crossing. She was three years older, sixteen to my thirteen years, and knew so much more about life. She knew about boys. Many of the boys on the ship seemed interested in her but she liked to spend time with me.

As the ship, an American troop transporter, plowed its way through the North Sea and entered the English Channel, the going began to get rough. As the boat rocked and swayed with the waves, so did our hammocks. More and more people became seasick.

The sound of retching and the stench of vomit drove us from our quarters. In the middle of the night Mutti dressed us warmly, grabbed me by the hand and dragged me up to an upper deck, where we could see the ocean and smell the fresh air. The air smelled wonderful, but the sight of the black ocean scared me to death.

Soon I too succumbed to seasickness. Night and day, the boat rocked back and forth; night and day I was nauseated. Mutti insisted she had the cure for this malady; all you had to do was look at the ocean. She marched me along the open deck from bow to stern and back again, admonishing me to look at the water. Whether we stood at the front or at the back of the ship, I was sure it was going to sink. At one moment you could only see the sky and the next the ship seemed to dive into the deep. But we marched on, up and down, up and down. Mutti's next attempt to stem my sickness was somewhat more successful .She made me suck on a lemon. I sucked and sucked until my mouth was puckered and my tongue was raw. The vomiting did stop only to give way to chronic nausea that lasted the entire remainder of the trip.

Meals were served in a huge dining hall, which had been the mess hall for the troops. Tall tables stood in long rows; there were no chairs. We had to stand at table to eat our meals. (I wondered, was this common for troops not to be allowed to sit down at table?) This went against my mother's lifelong rule never to eat standing up. In spite of her urging me to eat – standing up- I constantly felt disobedient. Mealtimes once again became a time of pleading and argument, compounded by feeling sick and nauseous with no appetite.

Two days into our ocean voyage, in the middle of a cool, sunny morning, I was playing cards with Malka and her friends on an outside deck. The ship's foghorn started to sound long repeated blasts. The only time I had heard this sound was when we left the harbor and that blast had signaled farewell. I was terrified. What did these long frantic blasts indicate now? It could only mean that something was wrong. The boat must be sinking! Soon members of the crew were instructing all of us to put on life jackets. People were running up and down the deck. In a short while, Mutti found me and we hurried down to our quarters where our life jackets were kept. My fear and panic brought on a sudden bout of diarrhea, so that going to the toilet further delayed putting on my life jacket and getting to our assigned life boat. I feared the boat would sink before I could wipe my bottom and get on my life preserver. We finally did get upstairs to our designated lifeboat, when we heard the shrill sound of whistles and shouts by the crew that the practice drill was over.

Our ocean crossing took nine long and stormy days and finally the announcement came over the loud speaker that we would be entering New York harbor soon. In great excitement and with huge relief that this trip was almost over, I looked for my mother so that we could go up on deck to catch the first glimpse of our new country. I looked everywhere but Mutti was not to be found. Finally someone told me that she was downstairs in the infirmary, which was off limits to me. My mother was one of the few passengers who had not gotten seasick. She had volunteered to help the overwhelmed infirmary staff tend to the many patients suffering from severe seasickness and other maladies. Not daring to break the rules by going in, I stood at the entrance of the infirmary, hoping to catch her attention when the door opened. I couldn't see her. Finally, feeling alone and dejected I went up on deck by myself.

Everyone was lined up at the rail, talking excitedly, pointing at the view. And what a sight met our eyes. In the distance you could see the skyline of New York, so many big buildings all blurred together. Then a small island came into view and on it stood a giant statue of a green lady. As the ship came closer I saw that she wore a crown, in one hand held a book and in the other a torch. Then I understood; this was the Statue of Liberty. There she stood in New York harbor welcoming us to our new country and where was Mutti? Suddenly my tears turned to sobs. I felt so terribly alone at this moving moment.

After the ship had sailed past the Statue of Liberty a series of small tugboats attached themselves to it and began towing it into the harbor. This took a long time; our ship must have been very heavy for these little boats. After a while there was an announcement over the loudspeaker informing all passengers to prepare for disembarkation. We would be landing soon. I scuttled back down to our quarters among crowds of excited people rushing every which way. Our bags had been packed the night before and stood ready. I still couldn't find my mother. At this point, I began to fear that I would have to disembark and walk down the gangplank into our new country all alone. Where was she? It was she who wanted to go to America, not me. Now that we were there, she was not. Just as my anxiety threatened to turn to extreme agitation, she rushed into the room, scolding me for getting so excited.

"Didn't you know that I had to help the sick people get ready? And didn't you know that I would be back in time? Now stop crying like a baby and help me up with the suitcases."

We joined the line of passengers snaking slowly down the gangplank into a crowded landing shed where we waited in line to see what to do next. There was much shoving and confusion. Eventually a woman with a very nice smile approached us. She wore a Red Cross uniform and tried to make conversation with my mother in English. Mutti pointed to me indicating that she could not speak English but that I could. The lady turned to me and asked what sounded like a question, because her voice went up at the end. But I couldn't understand. In my most polite English, I responded: "I beg your pardon?" She repeated her question not just once but three times, before she gave up and turned away. So much for my English comprehension; some spokesperson I turned out to be. To this day, I don't know what the nice Red Cross lady with the pleasant smile wanted to know. I do understand now that the formal King's English I had been taught did not sound at all like the English spoken here in America.

Upon leaving the disembarkation shed some passengers were met by friends or relatives, others by representatives from refugee organizations. I watched the tearful reunions with hopeful fascination. Would there be anyone to meet us? Suddenly my mother cried out and waved frantically to a bald man, who turned out to be Uncle Erich. He had come to meet us. He pushed through the crowd until he reached us, when he suddenly stopped, as if embarrassed. After a silent moment he and Mutti embraced tearfully, making me cry too. They had not seen each other for eleven years, not since Uncle Erich left Germany in 1938.

We took a taxi to Grand Central Station to catch a train to Worcester, Massachusetts. Through the windows of the taxi I peered at the hustle and bustle of the streets. So much noise and so many people. The buildings were so high I couldn't see the tops. Suddenly I was very tired and needed to close my eyes. Before we boarded our train, we had enough time to have a small meal in the station. I had never seen such a big restaurant and was not able to eat a bite. This time Mutti didn't even chide me to "eat something" as she usually did. A brief visit to the washroom in the station and then we would be ready to board our train. I removed my ring before washing my hands, a beautiful aquamarine set in a lovely white gold setting, given to me as a farewell present by my grandmother. Not until the train pulled out of the station did I glance at my hand and realized that I had left the ring on the sink of the washroom in Grand Central station in New York. Uncle Eric owned a jewelry store. He tried to soothe my despair with the promise of a new ring when we got to Worcester. True to his word, he gave me a gold ring with a yellow topaz. This was indeed a lovely ring, but not to my eyes. It could not compare to my beautiful lost treasure. Of course I didn't say that to Uncle Erich, but to this day I have not stopped searching for an aquamarine as deep blue and lovely as the one I lost.

Some weeks after we had arrived in Worcester, Massachusetts, we got notice to pick up our shipments. It had taken our duffel bags and boxes a very long time to make the trip. We went to the shipping office to pick them up. Everything was there, except one duffel bag. In spite of all efforts to trace it the bag was never found. In it were my Erika doll and my accordion.

As soon as Mutti managed to save up enough money, she bought me another accordion. Now I certainly didn't have the heart to tell her about my dislike for the instrument. She had bought me a beautiful instrument with her hard-earned money. It was shiny black and silver and had twenty-four bases, twice as many as the old German one. So I continued my lessons and practiced faithfully. As I played the American songs on my new accordion, I silently grieved for my poor, lost doll, my sister Erika. I guess they were right when they said that I was getting too old to play with dolls.

CHAPTER 18
FIRST DAYS IN AMERICA

WE ARRIVED IN WORCESTER ON OCTOBER 2, 1949. Uncle Erich took us to his home on Havelock Road on the 'West Side', which he explained was the more desirable part of town. We were to stay there until we were settled enough to be on our own. The family consisted of Uncle Erich, his wife, Aunt Ruth and their two little sons. Ken was seven years old and Mark just eighteen months. Aunt Ruth's mother and aunt, who had recently arrived after surviving a concentration camp, completed the family. The three bedroom house was full, but space was made for us in the sunroom where we slept on an open up couch. We were the first of many relatives whom my uncle sponsored and who used his house as a way station.

Our arrival coincided with the Jewish holiday of Yom Kippur. I was totally unfamiliar with this holiday and equally ignorant of the prohibitions which would soon be demanded of me in a very severe way. 'Grandma', Aunt Ruth's mother, was an austere old woman with snow white hair and a wooden leg. She had lost her real leg in an air raid in Germany. Every time she stood up or sat down she clicked the metal hinges on her wooden leg. She really scared me.

I was very hungry after the long train ride. When after several hours we had not been offered any food I timidly requested something to eat. Grandma scolded

"No, you can't have anything to eat. Don't you know that you have to fast today?"

Embarrassed and hungry, I quietly withdrew into a corner. It seemed that with every move I managed to offend Grandma. When I noticed that my skirt had a loose button I requested needle and thread. Grandma clicked her metal hinge, straightened her wooden leg, as she rose from her chair and reprimanded "No, I will not tell you where to find a needle and thread. Don't you know you are not allowed to sew today?" I was only trying to be neat and responsible the way Mutti had taught me. My initiation into the ways of Jewish behavior and expectations was harsh and frightening, conveyed by a very scary woman who reminded me of a witch.

My mother was now faced with the daunting challenge of making a new life for us in Worcester. She took employment as a live-in housekeeper, while I boarded with my aunt and uncle. She visited once a week on her day off but never raised the delicate matter of being Jewish. One night, Aunt Ruth came to my bed, sat down next to me, and gently said: "You know, Ingrid, now that you are living with us, you have to be like us. We are all Jewish and you have to be Jewish now too." Confused and frightened, but eager not to displease Aunt Ruth whose affection and approval I needed, I answered: "But I am a Catholic girl, and I don't know how to be Jewish." "It's not hard," Aunt Ruth pressed on. "We go to Temple on Saturdays and you will go with us. You will also go to Hebrew school. Then you will be Jewish like us." Confidently, she kissed me good night and left me in my bed to weep and worry over what would become of me.

I began to go to Hebrew school and tried to apply my previously established learning habits to this foreign effort which seemed to come so easily to all the other boys and girls. They had been learning these strange symbols and sounds for five years. I had been deposited in the sixth grade of religious school. I was lost; my already bleeding identity began now to hemorrhage dangerously. A private tutor patiently led me through the basic building blocks of learning this new alphabet and to translate a few words. I remember the first two words I learned were *yeled katan*, (little child). Indeed I felt like a very little child again, having to learn such basic but overwhelming things at thirteen.

I had always been a good student and was able to learn enough to fake it. I was actually allowed to participate in Confirmation of the Class of 1950. The photograph still hangs on the wall of Temple Emanuel's Hebrew School in Worcester to prove it. Now I was no longer a German Catholic girl, but an American Jewish one. Or was I? I was no longer certain about anything I was or wasn't but I had learned to meet external expectations. I had put Judaism on like I had put on hand-me-down clothes. Inside, I grieved for the familiar Catholic religious practices and beliefs that had always given me comfort and joy. This newly donned religion didn't go any deeper than sounds and behaviors. No one taught me the meaning and depth inherent in Judaism. I was spiritually starved for many years, in terrible pain about my duality, not knowing where I belonged or who I was.

At the same time, I needed to learn the language of my new country and was sent to Lamartine Street School where conversational English was taught to foreigners from various countries. They were all much older than I. We all struggled to learn English together. I was very comfortable here; I was not the only greenhorn.

Aunt Ruth took her new project of the 'Americanization of Ingrid' very seriously and personally. She was going to mold me into a proper American teenager speaking English without an accent. She had never been able to achieve this herself, having arrived in America as an adult and continued to speak with a substantial German accent. One day she decreed that I was no longer allowed to speak German in the house. Here I was, living in a three generation German speaking household, but when I spoke in German I encountered a deaf ear. I could only receive responses to my many questions if I labored them out in English. What torture! This did have the desired effect of learning English quickly, and eventually accent free.

My renovation continued with attention to hair and dress. Looking at my long, thick braids, Aunt Ruth proclaimed that "Here in America we don't wear our hair in braids. All the girls here have short, stylish hair. Tomorrow, we'll go to the beauty parlor and have your hair cut and set." My beautiful thick, ash-blond hair was my only source of pride and just the thought of a pair of scissors made me break out in a cold sweat. I wouldn't be Ingrid without my braids. I cried and pleaded to no avail and finally succumbed. The next day sitting in a swivel chair at the beauty parlor with a long gray cape around me, I closed my eyes when the operator approached with a pair of gigantic scissors. I felt the sound of the shears resonate in my whole body as the first braid was severed from my head and then the other. I slowly opened my eyes, shook my head back and forth feeling the strange lightness and collapsed in tears at the sight of my shorn head. Through my sobs, I pleaded to take my severed braids home, but that was not allowed. "They'll get lice", responded Aunt Ruth. "No, you can't possibly keep them; they'll lie in a drawer and breed vermin. Not in my house!"

"Then I'm not going home with you. I want my braids back," I sobbed. "I don't want them to be cut off, I don't want to leave them here, I don't want to look like an American girl; I don't want to be in America."

For a long time, I avoided mirrors and when I accidentally glimpsed my reflection, I experienced a queasy sense of disorientation. "Who is that girl? What happened to Ingrid?"

My identity was further undermined by Aunt Ruth's quest to transform me by Americanizing my wardrobe. Instead of the beautiful hand knitted skirts and sweaters so lovingly knitted by my mother in preparation for our trip, I now wore the hand-me-downs donated by my aunt's friends. Wool skirts and jackets discarded by their previous owners now hung shapelessly on my thin frame. Then it was time for a bra, and Aunt Ruth and I were off to the stores, returning home with a bag full of size 30 AAA bras. Embarrassed to wear these strange trappings, which did nothing to augment my stick- figure, I nevertheless obeyed my aunt to gain her approval for looking like an American girl. Although at heart I was …. actually, I wasn't sure anymore who I was.

My first Christmas in the new country was particularly difficult. During the day I met the outward requirement of appearing Jewish, but at night while quietly weeping in my bed, I ached with loss and loneliness. The time before Christmas had always been one of anticipation and excitement in Germany, even during the hardest times. It was always filled with religious and personal warmth and meaning. Even during my time in hiding when I couldn't leave my cell in the bunker, Oma had somehow managed to sneak in a little surprise while the sounds of Christmas music filtered under the door. Now in this new place where I had to pretend to be Jewish, Christmas was anathema. In the privacy of my bed, with tears of yearning wetting my pillow, I thought about the piney fragrance of a live Christmas tree lit with real candles and about the beloved and beautiful songs. Fervently recalling when Papi was still home and he and Mutti whispered together about secret surprises,

I yearned for the aroma of cookies baking in the oven and for the mystery and excitement of going to midnight services in the freezing cold. This was the only time my parents came to church. Summoning up the memory of the excitement of gifts under the tree, I recalled the Christmas when Erika, who would become my childhood companion, waited there for me. Another year, the first Christmas after our return home, I received a large blackboard on an easel for playing school. Most memorable of all, at a time when imported goods were unheard of, there was a giant orange. I saved this precious object until it was dry and shriveled up and had to be thrown away. With these sweet memories, I soothed myself to sleep in my lonely bed in this confusing new place, making sure there were no visible tears of sadness in the morning when I had to face the family.

Many things in this new world were different and astounding. I was filled with amazement at the foods served every day. The plates were too full with so many unfamiliar foods. Bread was snow white and came already sliced in a clear bag and then they even spread butter on it. They ate meat with their potatoes and vegetables every single day. I felt full just looking at all that food. There was a fruit shaped like a large yellow ball, called grapefruit, which was promised to be a great delicious treat. But when I allowed myself to be persuaded to try one, I didn't like it at all. It was bitter and sour and didn't taste like grapes at all. There was also a food eaten for breakfast that was truly strange. They poured something pebbly from a box into a bowl, added sugar and milk and ate it with a spoon; they called it cereal. This concoction actually didn't taste bad at all; in fact I came to like it, especially with small pieces of banana cut in. One day my uncle offered me a banana, the first banana I ever ate. I took a knife and tried to figure out how to peal it, accompanied by laughter around the table. "Dummy, you don't use a knife to peal a banana! Ha-ha-ha-ha."

So many things were strange. Some of the groceries were kept in a big, closet-like container, called a refrigerator. It was shiny white, and you opened it by pulling on a large chrome handle. Inside it was lit up with an electric light. It had shelves for food and even some drawers. It was very cold inside and all the food was very cold. One evening while the family was at the table for dinner, my aunt asked me to get the bottle of milk from the refrigerator. After I placed the milk on the table my uncle asked: "Did you check if you turned off the light in the refrigerator?" When I opened the door again and couldn't figure out how to turn it off, I was again met with roars of laughter. I never quite forgave them; how was I supposed to know that the light went off when you closed the door.

These were the days I discovered cookies and started a lifelong love affair. These crunchy, sweet and ever so enticing confections came in never ending variety. Shaped in little circles or squares, single or double layered, some were filled with creamy fillings flavored in vanilla, lemon or chocolate, some with icing on top or without. I simply couldn't get my fill. A lot of things in America were strange and incomprehensible, but cookies - - - they were a wonder.

CHAPTER 19
LIFE IN AMERICA

AFTER THREE MONTHS LEARNING ENGLISH AT LAMARTINE Street School it was decided that I was ready to enter Classical High School. My first days there passed in confusion. I had never seen so many students in one building. I was given a card with my schedule of courses replete with times and room numbers. I was on my own, although totally overwhelmed and baffled. Students were rushing up and down the stairs to get to their classes. I stood among them with tears streaming down my cheeks not knowing where to go. Eventually a teacher asked me why I wasn't going to my class. In my despair, my English failed me completely. The man looked at my schedule, took me by the arm and led me up the stairs to my math class. I don't remember how I got through the rest of the day.

For the rest of the semester, I tried to make myself as invisible as possible sitting in the last row and slouching low in my seat in terror of being called on. I was shy and quiet, living out the old adage of being seen and not heard, when one day the history teacher called on me with a question. I could no longer avoid being heard. My answer elicited a chorus of raucous laughter from the rest of the class. I had apparently mangled my English pronunciation or may have chosen a wrong word. I can still feel my red hot face. Desperately wanting to escape from the room, run out of school, or at least crawl under my desk, I instead just closed my eyes and burned.

With the intention to make the first year of high school a

little lighter for me, my guidance counselor had advised that I take German, which would require little effort leaving me free for the harder subjects. But in reality, it was quite a challenge. I was not accustomed to thinking of German as foreign language; conjugations, declensions, tenses! I just spoke my native language naturally. Our teacher, Miss Woodis, was delighted to have a genuine German student in her class and would regularly turn to me for validation. I would simply nod and smile politely. One day, however, she said something that was clearly wrong and once again she turned to me for affirmation: "Isn't that right, Miss Kammen?" What was I to do? Remain polite and tell a lie or be truthful? Getting nervous as she stared at me waiting for a response, I blurted out: "No, Miss Woodis; the right way to say it is:......." Miss Woodis turned pale and remained rigidly still as a communal gasp of shock was heard from the rest of the class. Then she walked to the other side of the classroom and continued the lesson. Miss Kammen was no longer asked to verify the correctness of the teacher's German after that.

In my homeroom period, a girl named Shanie adopted me as a friend. We sat together in the lunchroom and walked together to the bus at the end of the day. She didn't laugh at me and we managed to make ourselves understood. Shanie explained to me about sororities and saw to it that I was invited to pledge for hers. The whole process of pledging made little sense, but I was slowly starting to have some fun. Wearing two different color socks to school was good for some chuckles, as was having to carry around a raw egg for a day without breaking it. When I was inducted, I suddenly had a whole group of girl friends. We giggled a lot, mostly about boys. Without being aware of it, my English was improving because I was speaking it without self-consciousness.

In the meantime my mother had progressed from being a live-in housekeeper. She had taken some courses and became what was then termed a practical nurse.. After acquiring a full time job nursing a terminal cancer patient, she subleased a bedroom from a family across the street from her job and we were able to live together again, albeit frugally. It was at this time that my mother started to date men. I was very angry about this, still secretly waiting for my father. I was looking out of the window of our single room one evening right after my mother had left on a date and saw her kissing the man. Convulsed with anger and nausea, I wouldn't speak to her for days. I wonder if she noticed. This was a particularly stressful time for our relationship. I missed Aunt Ruth's softer and more maternal ways. One day after a little squabble with my mother, she stated: "I don't know what has happened to you; you're just not the same child you were in Germany."

On the day of my fourteenth birthday, I had an unexpected surprise. I found a red stain in my panties and knew that this was my first period, something I had been waiting for to validate my adolescent normalcy. All my friends had had their periods for a long time and I was afraid that there was something wrong with me, maybe from the war. So when I saw the welcome stain I felt both frightened and relieved. Since my mother had always been too uncomfortable and avoided any questions I had about sexuality, I turned to my aunt instead. She gave me instructions on where and how to buy and use sanitary napkins. When my mother learned about this, she appeared to feel hurt and angry that I hadn't come to her.

When I started to date at age fifteen, like 'a normal American girl', my naïveté and lack of knowledge could have gotten me into real trouble had it not been for Jerry, one of my early dates. Parking on Grafton Hill after a movie, Jerry suddenly stopped kissing me; proof that he found me ugly, not properly American. As it turned out, Jerry was a really nice guy, who in spite of his hormonal urgings, did not want to take advantage of me. He confessed that he had asked me out because it was rumored among his peers that I was 'easy' because I was a foreigner. "You really have to learn how to say no, Ingrid," he added kindly. "Let me drive you home now."

I was now sixteen years old, old enough to have a boyfriend. Sheldon and I were well suited in that we were both very shy and decided to comfort ourselves in our social awkwardness by *going steady*, to the consternation of his family. Ours was a comfortable, innocent relationship. Sheldon was the second son of an orthodox Jewish family with seven children. There was something so appealing to me about his home and family. The large house was cluttered with toys, plants and Jewish ritual objects. It was a lived-in home, where there was a place to play for all the children, a place that spoke of love and comfort. Shabbat and holidays were strictly observed as were daily prayer and ritual. People seemed to take joy in it, even the little children. There was one thing, however, that puzzled me. How was it that Sheldon's mother had a new baby every year? There were seven children in the family already, and in my house I was the only child. When Sheldon asked me to attend his synagogue, I was aghast and frightened. I was told that women and girls had to sit in the balcony while he would be sitting downstairs with the men. Then I discovered that this synagogue, which was actually conservative, had a mixed choir and that they were seeking new voices. Now this was familiar territory, I knew how to sing. In this manner I managed to resolve my quandary. Having tried out for the choir and been accepted, I sang with them every Friday evening, thereby attending synagogue in my own way.

Nobody had to know what a dummy I was about Judaism. I was able to fake the Hebrew of the songs sufficiently after hearing them a few times. It has always been easier for me to learn lyrics in any language with music. Sheldon and I broke up when I was eighteen years old under pressure from his family who thought we both needed to see other people.

In 1951, my mother decided to get married again, a huge blow to me. Her patient had died and after a suitable interval, Max, the widower, and my mother agreed to marry each other. I was fifteen years old, still secretly hoping my father would return and find us one day and struggling with the conflicts of my own budding sexuality. I was very upset, but had no say in the matter. The upside was that we would be moving into our own house and that for the first time in my life, I would have a room of my own, which was further sweetened with the bedroom furniture of my choice. In retrospect, I acknowledge what a good marriage this was for my mother. It lasted twenty-five years, until Max passed away.

Max was an observant Jew and a kosher butcher who took his religious obligations seriously. On Friday afternoons, he would come home from work early. His mood was always cheerful then, as he got ready to take his weekly bath. He actually sang while he was soaking. We would eat Shabbat dinner in the dining room, where my mother had lit the candles. Often there would be other relatives joining us and the atmosphere was festive. Max said *Kiddush* (blessing over the wine) and cut the *challah* (Sabbath bread). On Saturday morning, he walked to synagogue, carrying his *tallit* (Prayer shawl) in its beautiful velvet bag. Before he left, I often heard a short discussion between him and my mother. Max trying to persuade her to come with him, my mother responding with reasons why she couldn't, such as having a headache or needing to get a hot lunch on the table. Once in a while mostly on the high holidays, she would relent and go with him, only to return home in an hour or so. Mutti clearly was not too eager to go to synagogue. She did, however, try to run a proper Jewish home for her new husband, with separate dishes and utensils for meat and dairy, cooking only the kosher meat Max brought home from the butcher shop.

There was something about Max's religious values and behavior that both fascinated and confused me. He had an attitude of authenticity and sincerity that appealed to my spiritual nature, but without grounding in Jewish law or tradition, it was strange and confusing.

Week by week and season by season, my experience of living in a Jewish household began to make its impressions on me. On Passover, the extended family joined us for the Seder, which Max ran with fervor and conviction. To this day, the sound of his voice invoking the traditional phrases of the *hagadah* (Passover prayer book) in Hebrew, none of which I understood, still echo in my memory complete with melodies. And when it came time to sing the songs together, even Mutti joined in with enthusiasm. How did she know them? Did she sing them in her parents' orthodox home when she was young? This was a side of my mother I knew nothing about. Any questions I attempted were brushed aside.

While in High School, I was finally able to pursue my love for singing again. I joined the Glee Club and Chamber Chorus. Later I became a member of the Worcester County Light Opera Company. Along with the other *sisters, cousins and aunts* of the chorus, I happily frolicked to the tunes of *Pinafore, Mikado* and other Gilbert and Sullivan confections. I had a dream all my childhood to become an opera singer when I grew up, an ambition that followed me to America. One day, my mother, who had been struggling hard to support us, surprised me. "I have found a singing teacher for you who will be flexible with his fees." I was exultant at the prospect of lessons and that my mother had remembered and honored my dream.

With excitement and nervous anticipation, I telephoned the teacher, shyly telling him of my wish to study voice. He asked a few questions and made an appointment at his studio the next week. Judging by the sonorous tones of his telephone voice I pictured him to be six feet tall, dark and handsome like all opera heroes. The great day arrived. The man who opened the door was short, portly and bald. My heart sank with girlish disappointment. But when he sang, he became my hero. His clear, mellifluous tenor voice demonstrated what beautiful singing was. At this audition, Mr. Heier concluded that I had a "pretty little soprano voice" that could be developed with maturity and careful training. We agreed on weekly lessons for a fee of $1.25 per hour which is what I could afford from my part time sales job at Lerner Shops. I was just seventeen.

Some months later, due to my new vocal confidence and no small amount of hubris, I brazenly overcame my shyness and auditioned for a part of the upcoming production by the Worcester County Light Opera Company of *The Chocolate Soldier*. For the judges, I sang *The Lass With The Delicate Air* in a steady voice but trembling knees. They offered me the female lead. Joyfully, I announced the news to my singing teacher at our next lesson. Mr. Heier became solemn and silent and gently told me that he could not allow me to accept the role, that I was not yet ready and it was his responsibility to protect my voice. I couldn't believe his words; didn't he know how much this meant to me? I was disappointed, hurt and angry but gave up the role. It took years before I could appreciate my teacher's nurturing sense of responsibility toward me and my vocal development.

In January 1954, I finished High School. Because graduation would not take place until June, I never attended; it seemed anticlimactic. My academic record was strong and I had a burning desire to go to college. My mother's response was inimical to the time: "You don't need college, you'll get married soon." The second part of my mother's words turned out to be prophetic, but the powerful desire burned on. I realized that lack of funds was part of the issue and determinedly applied for and received a scholarship from the Council of Jewish Women, enough to attend Becker Junior College for an Associate Degree for the first of two years. I loved the challenge of learning, but after a year, the money ran out. When all attempts at raising more money for the second year's tuition failed, I had to give up my hopes for a college education. I took a job as a typist at Harrington and Richardson rifle manufacturers and absolutely despised the job. The dream for a college education, however, remained alive for *someday*.

In November of 1954 my mother and I experienced a momentous occasion when we received our American citizenship among a hundred or so other hopefuls. The whole extended family was there to see us sworn in after which we went to a restaurant to celebrate.

Chapter 20
Too Young to Marry

I WAS EIGHTEEN YEARS OLD WHEN I met the man who would become my first husband. We were introduced by his aunt, a friend of the family. Steve was in the army in boot camp at Fort Devens. He was lonely and was looking to meet *a nice Jewish girl.* Too soon we began to go steady and went out every weekend he could get off the base. I was the envy of my friends. Not only was he good looking and dapper in his army uniform, but he was from New York. In provincial Worcester, that was reason for prestige. We decided to get married the following year. He was twenty years old to my nineteen. So young! (He actually needed his parents' written permission to get a marriage license.) I wonder to this day why my mother didn't counsel me against marrying too young. I suspect she was relieved to have me married.

Upon Steve's discharge from the army, we moved to Brooklyn, New York, where his father helped him get work in his trade. I was already six months pregnant. Apartments were hard to get, but his parents had managed to convince the super to let us have an available two and a half room apartment in their building. When we went with them to look at the apartment, my mother-in-law warned me to close my coat to disguise my pregnancy in case this might bias the super against us. We got the apartment and lived in these tight quarters, eventually with two children, for five years. Steve worked nights as a mailer for a newspaper and slept during the day. This put great strain on a young marriage with a baby in a small apartment. After our second child was born two and a half years later, we moved to a tiny attached house in Queens.

I was totally and happily involved in my role as a mother. Wendy and Ellen were miracles from heaven and completed me in a way nothing ever had. One stage of their life was more gratifying than the next. When they started school, it was a challenge for me to let them go. I was a loving, but overprotective mother. The marriage quickly became strained under its burdens. Steve worked nights, so it became my responsibility to try keeping the house quiet during the day when he slept, not an easy feat with two active little ones.

During the long years of this tense marriage, my spiritual development was stalled. I had mistakenly counted on my husband's religious background and training to further help me with mine. Unfortunately, he rebelled against his orthodox upbringing and abandoned all Jewish observance. When our two daughters grew to the age when I wanted to provide them with a Jewish education, I pleaded to join a synagogue, which he adamantly refused to do. This caused me great distress, since I wanted my children to have a secure identity and sense of belonging, both of which I had been deprived of. I did not yet have the inner strength to fight him for it and I still feel a huge sense of despair over this.

When our children were at the age I was during the Holocaust I began to suffer from anxiety and depression. The defenses that had thus far held me together began to crumble. Upon the urging of a good friend, I searched for help and began the long trip to recovery in therapy. I was fortunate in finding a wonderful psychoanalyst who was not daunted by my Holocaust experiences and helped me to thoroughly explore and heal my childhood suffering.

As the years passed, the strains on the marriage increased. With the help of years of good psychotherapy my autonomy increased, which was very threatening to my controlling husband. He eventually succumbed to alcoholism and after both of our daughters were educated, established in careers and married, I ended the marriage with divorce. Some time prior, I had pursued my old dream of a college education, and had returned to school, acquiring a Bachelors degree at Brooklyn College and a Master of Social Work degree from Adelphi University School of Social Work. Now, I was prepared to work and support myself.

CHAPTER 21
FREEDOM

AFTER I FINALLY HAD THE COURAGE TO end my difficult marriage, I experienced a wonderful sense of freedom in all directions. I matured in my skills as a social worker, and began to get tremendous satisfaction from my work. I had chosen a position that focused on the prevention of abuse and neglect of children in their families. I threw myself into my work heart and soul, not yet aware that helping these children also helped to heal my old wounds.

I bought and moved into the very first home of my own, a co-op apartment upon which I lavished much love and care. Free now to decorate it exactly as I wanted, in no time I began to appreciate the solace of my own refuge. The fear of being homeless had haunted me during the divorce process. Now I felt secure and happy in my new home, and proud of owning it.

Music again filled my life as I sang in the Great Neck Choral Society, and attended many concerts with my friends. This too was a freedom long forsaken. I went to a weeklong choral institute in the Berkshires, where my musicianship developed further and I experienced new friends and much joy in singing.

But most of all, I now felt free and ready to pursue the nurturing of my soul and joined a small Reform Temple around the corner from my new home. Self-conscious as a single woman, I was welcomed warmly into the congregation. In this relaxed and supportive atmosphere I was able to immerse myself freely in religious learning and practice. Friday evenings were celebrated with Shabbat services and for the first time in my life, I began to light candles. I took every available opportunity to study and learn, including Sabbath afternoon discussion meetings at the homes of newly found friends. These lovely afternoons when study and discussion were concluded with *Havdalah* (concluding prayers) that wonderful ritual of ending the Sabbath and beginning the new week, were memorable experiences. I will never forget the experience of my first Yom Kippur in my new congregation, when I fasted for the first time in my life and spent the day with my fellow Jews at synagogue all day. At the end of the day, I experienced a spiritual exhilaration not felt since childhood. Soon I joined the choir at temple, but now when I sang the beautiful songs in the ancient language of the Jews, I learned their meaning and loved them for their content. My hunger for learning was boundless and I made the commitment to join an Adult Bat Mitzvah class. For two years, we engaged in intensive study with the rabbi. When the Bat Mitzvah celebration was scheduled for October, 1988, I did not yet feel sufficiently prepared and chose not to participate. I needed to learn more and grow further spiritually. Even though I had gained an immeasurable amount of information about Judaism, I did not yet feel authentic. Then I joined Project Identity (the name sounded like just what I needed) a curriculum of Jewish Studies at a local modern orthodox synagogue. There I took courses in Bible, Holiday Practices, and Hebrew Language. The choices were endless.

"Are you ready for the singles scene?" asked my lawyer as first I and then my almost ex-husband signed the separation agreement. In a year, our divorce would automatically become final. It had been a long, tortuous process, but now I was free – a little disoriented, a little scared – but free. "This calls for a celebration" I said to myself "and what better way to celebrate than to buy a new outfit." In the upscale boutique into which I would previously never dare to set foot, I drifted toward a rack of brightly colored slacks instead of the usual black, brown or beige which my previous conservative self would have favored.

One hour later, I walked out with a shiny shopping bag filled with wads of tissue paper, a pair of buttercup yellow slacks and a magnificent frilly white blouse. I felt as if I was floating six inches above the sidewalk and my heart was filled with a song of joy. Starting to hum under my breath, I soon began to sing out loud, not caring for once what passersby thought of me

"Are you ready for the singles scene?" I repeated to myself. Knowing I would never be ready, I decided to do the counter-phobic thing; tonight, I would go to that singles program at Temple Beth El I had seen advertised. I would break the ice before my fear would catch up with me. After all, the program was about music and I could pretend to myself that I didn't care about meeting men; that I was just there to enjoy the music.

That evening, checking myself in the full length mirror, I decided that the crisp white tailored cotton dress flattered my newly slimmed down figure. (The anxiety of going through a divorce had melted the fat off my hips.) Something else was needed to brighten me up, to detract from the lines and wrinkles on my 49 year old face. Rummaging through the drawer I found the blue and green silk scarf which did the trick. Jauntily I draped it around my neck.

After parking the car and walking toward the temple, I felt a little shaky in the legs; perspiration dripping down my sides and my breath coming in short gasps. "Stop it," I admonished, "there's nothing to be nervous about. You're only here to get the first time over with, its not as if you're looking for a man, you only just got rid of one." I took three deep breaths which calmed me; thank God for Yoga training. Bravely heading for the entrance I felt a disconcerting tickle on my nose, chin and forehead after walking through a spider web. Hastily wiping my face with a handkerchief, I entered the meeting room.

Suddenly my courage deserted me and I had to fight a powerful urge to turn around and run. The room was filled with groups of people who were standing around in small segregated groups, women on one side and men on the other. A flood of panic familiar from my old inhibited days suffused me. Summoning all the effort of will I could muster, I walked over to a group of women and attempted to join the conversation. Looking me up and down, they ignored me and turned back into their circle, probably for the purpose of shutting out the competition. Fighting the now even stronger urge to run out of the room, I stalked over to the refreshment table on shaky legs, picking up a pretzel in order to have something to hold on to. I found my gaze drawn toward a man standing alone on the other side of the table with a cup of coffee in his hand. He was of medium height, slim and lithe looking, wearing an open neck shirt under a beige jacket which suited him well. I felt a magnetic pull. What was it that drew me so? Was it his beautiful white head of hair or maybe his open friendly gaze? As if impelled by an external force, I walked over to him and mumbled "There's no one to talk to here, all the people are standing around in knots." His beautiful smile widened in welcome as we effortlessly began a conversation, a conversation that still continues twenty-five years later.

CHAPTER 22
BEAUTIFUL MUSIC

I watched the telephone and silently willed it to ring. He had taken my number when we said good night forty-eight hours ago, the night of our meeting, when we had discovered that among other things we shared a profound love for music. I had noticed that when the featured violinist had offered tickets for an upcoming recital at Carnegie Hall, Jack, for that was his name, had rushed to accept two of them. Finally he called and invited me to dinner on Saturday night.

I spent much of Saturday rehearsing how I would offer to pay my share, for my newly born independent spirit demanded it. We arrived at the Spanish restaurant to the strains of a Flamenco tune. I learned later that he had carefully researched that the restaurant would have live music. We ordered paella, which we barely tasted, so intent were we on continuing the conversation that had begun four nights ago. There was so much to say. When we returned to my apartment, I regretfully explained that I was unable to invite him in because my daughter and son in law were visiting and were asleep in my living room. After a cool peck on the cheek, he took his leave stating he would call some time. Weeks later, he admitted that he had not believed me; he thought that I might be a cold fish and that he had better preserve some distance. He stayed distant for exactly two days, when he called to ask me to a violin recital at Carnegie Hall. This was quickly followed by a Sunday afternoon at the Beethoven Festival replete with a romantic picnic on the grounds of the Arboretum. The conversation resumed pianissimo between sonata movements, continued at mezzo forte at the end of a concerto and persisted at forte during the entire romantic picnic under the giant red beech tree sheltering us like an umbrella from onlookers.

This time I invited him in for a nightcap. The conversation resumed only to be briefly silenced when after a few shy kisses, we realized the full range of dynamics from piano to fortissimo. So began his weekly weekend sleepovers and his discovery that I was hardly a cold fish.

After four lovely years of 'courting', Jack Elefant and I decided to make a permanent commitment. On March12, 1989, we were married by a rabbi under a chuppah(wedding canopy),- surrounded by family and friends. Jack and I exchanged our wedding vows and listened with awe as the beautiful strains of the seven marriage blessings were chanted for us. At our reception, we chose 'September Song' to dance our first dance to. It resonates of the late in life love we have for each other.

But before the wedding could be held, two things needed to happen. Jack had to provide his first wife with a *get* (a Jewish divorce decree), and I had to acquire a Jewish name. (I had never been given one.) The first matter was completed expeditiously with the rabbi's referral to a *Beit Din* (a Jewish Court). The second took more thought. The matter of acquiring a Jewish name was a profound matter for me. A name connotes identity, it tells who you are. The rabbi had said he could give me one or I could choose one myself. I opted for my own choice, selecting the name of *Rut*, from the story of Ruth and Naomi. Hadn't Ruth been the first Jew by choice? I identified strongly with her. So with a few words by the Rabbi, I became *Ruth Bat Avraham v' Sheva*, (Ruth, daughter of Abraham and Sheva.) Abraham, the father of the Jewish people became my father too (since my biological father was not a Jew) and my mother's name was Sheva. My Ketubah hanging on our bedroom wall to this day attests to my new identity every time I look at it.

Throughout our now twenty-one year old marriage, Jack and I firmly believed that our meeting was destined, and that God had a hand in our meeting at just the right time. Coming from a traditional background, Jack quietly practiced his Judaism with an authenticity and integrity that enthralled me. Not making any demands on anyone but himself, he provided a role model and an environment in which I could freely pursue and learn my own authentic Judaism at my pace and in my way. Patiently he bore with me and gently corrected my mistakes, as I learned the Friday evening prayers in my stumbling Hebrew. I took delight in lighting Shabbat and holiday candles with him at my side. After our marriage, we joined a large conservative synagogue, where the opportunities for study are endless. I studied Hebrew and immersed myself in the history of my newly found people. Little by little I increased my ritual participation, gradually learning the joy and serenity of observing the Sabbath. Friends and family speculated that my newfound religion was to please Jack, but Jack and I knew otherwise. This was a natural evolution of spirit long suppressed. I was beginning to experience a sense of identity from belonging to an ancient people and tradition of which I had been deprived for so long.

One Saturday morning while at synagogue with my husband reciting the silent *Amidah* (standing prayer) along with the rest of the congregation, I was suddenly overcome with a most profound sense of connection. In my mind's eye, I could see Jews all over the world, praying these same ancient words. I saw an endless chain of people reaching back and back in time for thousands of years, all the way to Abraham, Isaac, and Jacob; to Sarah, Rebecca and Rachel and Leah. They were my people.

My husband turned to me at the conclusion of the *Amidah* and when he saw tears cascading down my cheeks wanted to know what's wrong. I responded, "Absolutely nothing; everything is just right."

L'DOR V'DOR

I stand in prayer
Surrounded by pray-ers
Silently intoning
Ancient words of blessing and supplication

I stand transported
In time and in space
As ancient words bind me
To my people

An unending chain
Not to be broken
Abraham, Isaac and Jacob
Sarah, Rachel, Rebecca and Leah
Sheva and Ruth.

Ingrid (Ruth) Epstein Elefant

Chapter 23
The Turning Point

For almost 59 years I had been carrying a weighty secret in my soul, a secret that took up more and more space inside me as the years passed, absorbing dreams, hopes and vital energy into itself. I was convinced that if anyone learned of my origins and early childhood, I would become a pariah. When our good friend, Rabbi Charry, who knew not only about my childhood circumstances but also my extreme reticence to talk about it ,gently asked if I might consider talking to our synagogue congregation at the upcoming *Yom Hashoah* (Holocaust Remembrance Day) commemoration, my immediate response was negative. "Impossible!" cautioned my internal voice. "If they find out who I really am, a Catholic German whose father was part of Hitler's army, a fraud who now masquerades as a Jew…I will never dare to show my face here again." Rabbi Charry, as if he had heard my inner dialogue, soothingly continued: "You are among friends here. Think about it, sleep on it. Who knows?" This was in March of 1997. In spite of myself, I began to entertain the possibility. My feelings alternated between shy confidence and total terror. On the one hand, I saw myself telling my story in public and feeling accepted with a huge weight lifted from my soul, on the other, I was gripped by an ice cold sweat believing I would be judged as enemy, a fraud who deserved to be excommunicated and banned. Once the idea was brought up, however, it would not be denied. I began to struggle with putting my story on paper. I could always change my mind.

May 4th, the date of the commemoration was now only a few days away. The program had been printed and publicly distributed, detailing my name and photograph as one of two speakers. There was no way out now. Practicing my speech the evening before, I panicked, sobbing to my husband: "I can't do this, what was I thinking? Please call and tell them that I'm running a 104 fever, that I'm highly contagious and that I can't be there tomorrow." My good Jack, too smart to try to convince me, said: "Call them yourself and explain that you're too scared." This had the effect of giving me renewed determination to tough it through. I decided the speech wasn't right and proceeded to rearrange it until it no longer made any sense at all. I became hysterical again and tore up this latest fiasco and went to bed. Of course I didn't close an eye for hours, but when sleep finally came it was filled with nightmares of terror and abandonment.

Next evening, the Yom Hashoah program began with the usual march of survivors down the aisle of our synagogue. I was flanked on both sides by young students carrying candles, my knees shaking in fear about when my deception would be known. The first speaker was a Holocaust survivor who became an Israeli pilot transporting Ethiopians to Israel during "Operation Solomon". I listened with awe and fear; this was not only a "real" survivor but a hero. How could I speak after this, how? My mouth was dry, sweat ran down my sides and I was dizzy. This felt surreal. The next words penetrating my consciousness were: "And now Ingrid Elefant, who was born in Germany, will tell you of her experiences." As if in a dream I rose and walked to the pulpit accompanied by the loud drumming from the beat of my heart. I looked out at the packed sanctuary, unable to make a sound. Then I saw the front rows filled with children, boys and girls from the Hebrew School, whose eyes were fixed on me expectantly. I began to talk to them, telling them about a girl close to their age, a girl who had been frightened during the bombings of the war, a girl who had been brought up Catholic to protect her, a girl who had been hidden from the Nazis by her grandparents. I told them how sad this girl had been, how lonely when she was left alone with her grandparents. Her father was in the army and she didn't know where her mother was. I told them about how the little girl had figured out that she must have been very, very bad. Why else would she have been so abandoned? At the end I told them what a lucky little girl I had been that my grandparents had dared to hide me. And then I told them, unexpectedly off script, how lucky they were to be able to go to synagogue and have Shabbat and holidays, and to know that they were Jews, and could be proud of it.

When I ended the large room remained absolutely silent and the wide eyes of the children were still on me. Then came .... unending applause.

When people began to crowd around to ask me questions and to congratulate and praise my presentation, I felt like I was being enfolded by the arms of my congregation. They now knew who I really was and they accepted me. More important, I now knew who I was. A Jewish woman who had been deprived of her heritage during her childhood, who had been saved by her parents' decision to raise her Christian and by the courage of her paternal grandparents. That was the first of many testimonies. Once the flood gates were opened there was no stopping the flow of words. I became one of a cadre of survivors working at the Holocaust Resource Center of Temple Judea in Manhasset, where we engage repeatedly with groups of young people to tell them our stories and how we survived. These young people have a way of asking questions that go to heart of my own questions. I have learned along with them. I have spoken at many different venues, the combined synagogues of Port Washington, Great Neck South and Freeport High Schools, the Regional Office of the Social Security Administration and at the Lawyers and Judges Chapter of Hadassah. Instead of experiencing terror at being discovered as a fraud, with each sharing of my life story I feel more and more authentic and integrated. I see it as my obligation to provide testimony from the Holocaust as long as I have breath and strength to speak.

Chapter 24
Reborn

In two weeks, I was going to ascend the *bimah* (altar) to read from the Torah for the first time. I had been preparing for this moment for six months with the patient and firm guidance of my mentor, Cantor Raphael Frieder. I believed that I had finally discovered the means by which to experience myself as a qualified Jew. This was not a thirteen-year-old blithely preparing for her bat mitzvah. I was a mature, sixty-year-old woman, struggling hard to pronounce the holy words written in the ancient alphabet that goes in the wrong direction.

Over time I had acquired a sense of Jewish engagement and identity from regular synagogue attendance and the lighting of Sabbath candles. After safely surviving a particularly serious surgery, I had even committed to following the dietary laws, and converted my kitchen to kosher standards. Each time I said the blessings over the candles, or denied myself a now forbidden food, the sense of living with commitment to the Covenant was strengthened, as was my sense of belonging. My connection to the Jewish community and to my temple, where full participation of women is encouraged, grew stronger and stronger. And yet I felt a vague, unfulfilled yearning, a sense of time lost that demanded compensation. The years in which I was disconnected from my Jewish heritage needed to be redeemed.

One Saturday morning, God sent me my answer. It was time for the reading of the weekly Torah portion, and my ears perked up as I heard the ancient cantillations intoned by the voice of a woman. Week after week men chanted the Torah, as tradition had dictated for centuries; but this was a revelation. The word of God uttered in the mellifluous tones of a woman's voice and spirit stirred something deep within me. Later I spoke with Linda, the woman who had chanted the Torah reading so movingly and asked her how she came to do this. She told of the many hours of practice spent under the tutelage of Cantor Frieder. She inspired me and assured me that I could learn to do it too. She became my role model and support.

With encouragement from my husband and tutoring from Cantor Frieder, I stumbled through my first awkward efforts of putting together the difficult biblical Hebrew phrases with their appropriate cantillations. It was slow going, much like trying to speak two foreign languages at the same time. I prevailed and one day the cantor announced that I was ready for my first formal reading at services. I panicked and tried to convince him that his confidence was unfounded; but he was not to be dissuaded. He insisted I was ready.

My first Torah reading was to be from the Book of Exodus, Chapter 38, *Parashat* (Torah Portion) *Pekudei,* due to be read in four weeks. I practiced furiously night and day and reached a point in my reading where I felt more or less secure. I had learned the words, the phrases and the trope of my portion and understood their meaning. When I practiced chanting, it sounded beautiful to me. The gift of a pleasant voice had once again come to my aid. What was it then that still nagged at me? What gave me that feeling of uneasiness, that sense of *tumah,* of spiritual uncleanliness? Could it be that the effects of my childhood religion presented a barrier between Torah and me? Did the waters of my infant baptism require purging?

I came to the conclusion that what I needed was a ritual, a ritual of cleansing, before I dared to ascend to the Torah for the first time. Might a *mikveh* (a ritual bath) the waters of life, purify me? Might this ancient Jewish system of cleansing serve to wash the past from me? Yes, I would go to a *mikveh!* I had never been anywhere near such a place before; I had no idea where to find one. Anything I had ever heard about *mikveh* belonged to another world. I could imagine only dank darkness and secret whispers. My friend Paula, our Rabbi's wife, came to my aid. She directed me to what turned out to be a modern *mikveh* some fifteen miles from my home, which resembled nothing so much as a tastefully appointed beauty spa. Nervously I approached the person sitting at a desk, expecting an interrogation as to my reasons for coming here. But she only informed me of the cost for use of the facilities. After paying my fee I was shown to a private bathroom, replete with tub and shower, stacks of soft, white towels, a fluffy white terry cloth robe and every kind of cosmetic item imaginable. There was soap, shampoo, deodorant, bath powder and body lotion. There were jars of cotton balls and Q-tips, nail files and scissors, nailbrushes and hairbrushes and more.

The attendant showed me around and encouraged me to take plenty of time. She told me that when I was ready I should knock on the door that led to the ritual pool and she would assist me. She repeated: "Don't rush, take all the time you need", as if to make sure that I would be clean enough.

I had previously studied the laws and regulations for *mikveh* preparation. Not expecting to find such a clean and modern facility I had already taken a bath at home. I had soaked for the requisite twenty minutes. I had scrubbed every inch of my body, had cut all twenty finger and toe nails and had carefully removed any flaw or callus from my skin. If I was going to do this, I was going to do it right. I was clean. Still I felt like a fraud. I turned on the water tap in the bathtub and made splashing noises. I couldn't have the matron think that I was being inappropriate. Then I decided to take another shower as much to use up time as to calm my jittery nerves. Finally, I decided it was time.

Wrapping myself in the soft white terry robe, I slowly approached the door to the *mikveh*. My heart hammered in my chest and thoughts raced each other through my head. What on earth was I doing here? Convinced the woman on the other side would discover that I was a fraud, I imagined that she would turn me away with "baptized people can't use a *mikveh*." But I had come so far I couldn't turn back now, and I could think of no further way to stall.

With trembling legs, I approached the door to the 'inner sanctum', wondering what I would find on the other side. Lifting my right hand slowly, bending my index finger stiffly, I tentatively knocked on the door once, twice and then again. No answer. "I told you she thinks you're a fraud," I said to myself. "She's just going to keep you waiting in here until you go away." Then the door opened and a smiling woman bade me to come in.

I entered a lovely, bright room filled with the soothing green of living plants. The walls were covered with soft –hued tiles and broad steps graciously led into a small pool. There was a hushed air of solemnity and when the attendant instructed me, she spoke in a soft and solemn voice, having learned from me that this was my first *mikveh* experience.

All at once, I remembered my reason for being here.This was

the ritual by which I would become *taharah*, spiritually prepared to become an authentic Jew. I trembled all over as the enormity of this moment penetrated by being. As I descended the first step, then the second, and finally the remaining ones, cool water slowly rose higher and higher engulfing me up to my chin. It felt like millions of welcoming arms softly enfolded me. Slowly I bent my knees to submerge fully, thereby entering a dark, once familiar world that I had known before. Thoughts of the mother who had given me life came to mind. While immersed, I felt I had dwelt here forever. Strange that I, who had always been terrified of going under water, felt at home here.

When I reluctantly ascended from these waters my world felt changed. As if from a far distance, I heard the voice of the attendant declare: "Kosher!" I began to weep.

Apparently moved by my sobs and recognizing that something deeply spiritual had occurred she walked out to give me privacy. Slowly my sobs subsided as warm tears of joy and gratitude washed my face. I felt as if I had been embraced by my Creator and been reborn into a world of peace and belonging. "Kosher!" I was no longer defiled, no longer disconnected and alone. Suffused with a sense of deep tranquility I stepped out of the pool, dried and dressed myself and returned home.

Two days later in the synagogue, I ascended the *bimah* nervously, but secure in my sense of worthiness. Silently I asked God to be with me as I humbly chanted His words. Feeling strongly linked to my People, holding on tightly to the *Etz Hayim*, the tree of life that is the Torah, I began to chant: *"Eleh pekudei hamishkan."*

CHAPTER 25
EMBRACED AND ACCEPTED

ON THE HOLIDAY OF SIMCHAT TORAH 2010 our Temple Israel Community bestowed on Jack and me the highest honor available to synagogue members, that of *Chatan v' Kallah v' Torah* (bride and groom of the Torah). This occurs annually to denote the end of the cycle of torah reading, before it begins immediately again with the reading of the beginning , signifying that the torah goes round and round, with no beginning or end, forever telling us something new.

Overjoyed by this tribute Jack and I decide to read the relevant portion of the torah on that day, and prepared for it with intensive practice. When the big day came we walked slowly down the aisle, happily escorted by our adult children, to the jubilant song of Cantor Frieder bidding us to *Im'ru, Im'ru,*(to ascend to the bimah) for our honor. As he called us up by name, *Yacov ben Zalman v' Sarah v' Rut bat Avraham v'Sheva* (Jack, son of Solomon and Sarah and Ruth, daughter of Abraham and Sheva) I felt a deeply stirring emotion within me, which made the warm, joyous tears flow. I finally felt not only fully accepted and honored by my congregation, I was now deeply integrated into and a valuable part of my people, Am Yisrael.

Jack and I ascended the bimah, said the blessing over the Torah and proceeded to take turns in chanting the portion of *Zot Ha Bracha* (This is the blessing), the words spoken by Moses to his people just before he died. I have rarely been so moved by the words of the Torah, they are so fitting, considering that our honor went to as Elders of the congregation.

Congratulations came at us from all directions, as people shouted out joyfully, *Yashir Koach, Yashir Kochachacheh,* (strength to you). Suddenly the Cantor began to sing a lively song to which people spontaneously joined in dancing a *horah* (folk dance) around us in celebration.

The rest of the day was spent in joyful celebration with our children, friends and congregants. When my daughters told us "You made us proud of you" I felt redeemed. The old wound of not giving them a Jewish education in their childhood felt eased. I had had the opportunity to be a role model to them now. Not only did I feel like a good Jew, but also a good Jewish parent.

Chapter 26
Looking Back

Now that I am in my seventies, I look back at my early life from a different perspective. I feel deep gratitude to the people that helped to keep me safe. They gave me the chance to live my later years, both difficult and good, along with the opportunity to consolidate my identity and become integrated into the Jewish people. I can now see where my mixed religious background has given me the spiritual groundwork from which I could grow into a deeply spiritual person, content within Jewish ritual practice and community.

I had the chance to enjoy the freedom of this amazing country, even with its many issues. I lived to establish a family and raise two wonderful children. They have grown into strong, talented and loving women, who have raised families of their own. My grandchildren, Jason, Sarah, Joshua and Stephanie are my treasures and joy. In addition to being smart, beautiful, loving and accomplished, their existence is my triumph. Hitler did not succeed at wiping us out. *Am Yisrael Chai* (The people Israel live)!

My mother and I continued to have a difficult relationship, but she enjoyed a compatible second marriage for twenty-five years. With maturity I came to appreciate her strengths, and am grateful to have been the daughter of such a courageous woman. She was struck by a devastating stroke when she was 72 years old which sadly left her aphasic and hemiplegic for the last fourteen years of her life. I visited her grave recently where I experienced a great sense of serenity and peace, knowing that her suffering is over and that now she must be in *Gan Eden* (the Garden of Eden)

I eventually became reconciled to the reality that my father was really dead and then I felt the need to find a way to memorialize him ritually. Fortunately, my beloved Judaism provides the means by saying Kaddish at Yahrzeit. For several years now, I have commemorated my father by saying Kaddish at our temple on the anniversary of his death, ever since I learned that it was appropriate, even though he was Christian.

He was killed in World War II when resistance fighters in the mountains of Greece killed the members of his squad, just days before the fighting ended there. His body was never returned to us; he shares an unknown grave with his comrades in death. He was thirty-nine years old then and I was eight. In lieu of a funeral, a memorial service was held then at a Catholic church in his home town. Neither the chanted ritual of the requiem mass, nor the tears on the somber faces of my relatives served to convince me then that my father was dead. At that age, the only direct experience with death had involved my pet rabbit, for whom we had held a solemn funeral, complete with a tin box for a coffin, flowers and a carefully dug grave behind the chestnut tree. Visiting his little grave had helped me to come to terms with my bunny's death, (as did the acquisition of a new pet). For my father there was neither a funeral nor a grave.

Years later, with my gradual transformation into a mature woman, came not only the acceptance of the early death of my father, but also a need to commemorate it fittingly, to honor his life. One Saturday our rabbi spoke about his visits to various cemeteries, about those he had visited in foreign countries and how they provided not only dignified means of remembering the dead, but historical information as well. He lamented the desecration and destruction of sacred places during the holocaust, including synagogues and Jewish graves. He avowed that the most enduring sacred places and memorial markers are in the hearts of people when they gather as a community to say the *Kaddish* (memorial prayer) in memory of their dear ones. I am grateful to Rabbi Mordecai Waxman for the comfort he inadvertently gave me. Fifty-seven years after my father's death, I found peaceful closure with the knowledge that he has an enduring monument in my heart.

My grandparents died within a few years after we left for America. Opa went first and Oma followed soon after. A few years ago, I wrote the following letter on the walls of my heart to say my farewell and express my gratitude.

Dear Oma,

Now that I am the age you were when you took me in, cared for and protected me as a child, I think of you. How different we are from each other; you were a product of your time, I the result of mine. Yet I suspect we share more likeness than just our names. I must confess I have always had mixed feelings about my middle name, Agnes, your first name. It's so old fashioned and I admit with some shame, so Christian sounding. But I am also proud to be named for you in the belief that I inherited your strengths.

You were stern and sombe,r dressed in your long, unadorned black dress and high laced shoes. On Sundays you added a white lace collar and a single strand of coral. I was fascinated with your hair, worn in a bun on top of your head, held in place by thick hairpins and covered with a black paisley shawl when you went out. I would eagerly wait for you to begin your daily hair brushing ritual. You would pull out the pins, hold them in your mouth and let your abundant hair descend until it reached your waist. Then you bent forward until your hair hung down in a white curtain. Holding my breath I watched the brush glide through your hair again and again. I like to believe that I inherited my once thick hair from you, Oma; even though I have mine cut stylishly short.

You smiled only rarely, but when you did I loved to see your face crinkle up. Mostly though I remember you looking serious, your mouth pursed as you went about your daily work. Your house was filled with so many people at a time when you and Opa were entitled to some peace and quiet. It was a matter of course to help when your children and grandchildren needed you. Tante Lisbeth, your youngest, moved into your home with her two little boys, Klaus and Horst, after their father was drafted. Onkel Leo, your last unmarried son, also moved back when he became unemployed.

Without question you took me in and found a hiding place for my mother. How exhausting your labors were, so many people to care for, even without me in your home to protect from the claws of the Nazis who were intent on deporting all Jews to their death camps. What must it have been like for you to be burdened with such a dangerous responsibility? You had already lost your youngest son to the Third Reich. Onkel Franz, whom I never knew, was murdered after being arrested for handing out anti Nazi leaflets. Two more of your sons, one of them my father, were in the army. You did not know whether they were alive or dead. When the letters stopped coming from my father you suspected that he might be injured or dead. You must have been despairing but you never let it show.

Onkel Leo, angry and frightened that someone might find out that you were harboring me, a half-Jewish child, challenged you severely. I overheard him argue loudly with you one night when you all thought I was asleep. I was so shaken by his accusations that I was putting your lives in danger. I could not understand in what way I was dangerous. Your firm retort: "She is ours and she stays here. I never want to hear another word about it" comforted me and softened my fear. I resolved to always be good so you would be safe.

Oma, I never heard you complain about your responsibilities, nor saw the anxiety you must have endured. You stalwartly went about your daily work and made sure that the rest of us did ours. You kept after Opa to tend to his garden and to clean the rabbit cages. I think this must have been your way of caring about him, even though at the time I thought you were kind of mean to him. Opa and I were kindred spirits; both of us were quiet and shy, and tended toward daydreaming. When you made me do schoolwork at the kitchen table every day, so that I would not fall behind, I was sometimes resentful. Now I know that this was your way of taking good care of me. Because, when I finally did return to school after the war, I never skipped a beat in keeping up with my classmates.

When the air raids became too dangerous for us to continue to shelter in the cellar, you decided we must find a way to go to the public air raid bunker in order to be safe from the bombs. I realized years later that you and Opa had stayed in the cellar with me so nobody would know you were hiding me and how dangerous this was to your own safety. Somehow you managed to smuggle me into the bunker without discovery and into the cell that was assigned to your household. You warned me sternly never to attempt to leave the cell nor to make a sound, without explanation. How could you explain the dangers of the Holocaust to an eight year old? Again I found you severe.

Today I know you saved my life with your stern love and your courage.

Then the war was finally over and I left your care after my mother had safely returned from her own hiding ordeal. I never gave a thought to how you might feel about my joy at my mother's return and my eagerness to leave you. Soon Tante Lisbeth also moved back to her own home with her two boys, and Onkel Leo got a job and moved to his own apartment. You and Opa were alone again. Were you relieved to have your quiet home back? Did you feel a little abandoned and lonely? We did visit you after that, but these were only short visits. The only time I ever saw you cry was during our last visit. I was thirteen and my mother and I would shortly be immigrating to America. You sat me on your knee, tenderly stroking my hair, pleading with me not to go. "I know I will never see you again" you wept.

*You were right Oma; you and I never did see each other again. Five years after settling in America a somber announcement, outlined in black, formally declared your demise. It said that you had passed away peacefully and that you were survived by three children and nine grandchildren. I was one of the nine. Some time later I received a small sum of money, my part of your modest estate. Recalling your coral Sunday necklace I bought myself an antique gold pendant with a small coral rose in its center with my inheritance. It always reminds me of you. My material inheritance may have been modest, Oma; but you left me a moral legacy without measure. By protecting me and safeguarding my life in that time of terror, you imbued me with a sense of loving responsibility for others, a value that continues to fill my living with meaning. You have shown me how a woman can have tenderness as well as strength and courage. Oma you were truly **A Woman of Valor.***

OMA AND OPA

Farewell to Oma

A challis scarf once draped her head
Black, soft and yellow paisley.
Immodest to walk outdoors uncovered

I stole it from her drawer
To drape my sad cold heart,
Lamenting her farewell.

Ingrid Epstein Elefant

About the Author

Ingrid Epstein Elefant was born in Germany during the Nazi regime and survived by being raised Christian and eventually in hiding. After the war Ingrid moved to the United States, where she married, raised a family and pursued a gratifying career as a clinical social worker.

She lives in Great Neck, N.Y. with her husband.

CPSIA information can be obtained at www.ICGtesting.com
Printed in the USA
BVOW020937311212

309230BV00001BA/93/P